Many have benefitted from the ministry of the Rev. William Philip. His pastoral experience, as well as his skill in opening up the Word of God, is evident in this set of reflections on six Psalms. We are able to come to God with heartfelt worship, thanksgiving and devotion, as well as lament and hope. Our spiritual life is enriched by the Psalms with their emotional range and relevance to every season of life.

Sharon James
Social Policy Analyst, The Christian Institute

Once a potato chip (= crisps) manufacturer pitched its product with: 'Betcha can't eat just one!' I think that is Willie Philips's design with these Psalms: to give us a taste and hook us on the Psalms. His let-me-give-you-just-a-taste approach is clearly sneaky but completely proper. No dodging nasty questions, nothing superficial here; just solid, 'thought-full,' nourishing exposition in perfectly lucid prose. (And don't you dare pass up his treatment of Psalm 88).

Dale Ralph Davis
Former Minister-in-Residence, First Presbyterian Church,
Columbia, South Carolina

This gem of a book provides rare medicine for the soul amid all the changing scenes of life. Expounding six very varied psalms, Dr. Philip builds bridges from the biblical text directly into the believer's heart to enable God's truth to accomplish its purposes of comfort and challenge, in both knowledge and practice. With commendable honesty about life in the real world, these expositions are wonderfully God-centred, building faith and so transforming perspectives. This is biblical preaching at its best – exegetically profound, pastorally warm-hearted an'... my heart good!

Past Pr<

T0016969

When you realise the world is a frightening and evil place, the Psalms are a great place to go. In this book William Philip offers thoughtful meditations on six key Psalms for our reflection and encouragement. It has got me reading the Psalms more, where I have found much comfort and strength. I'm glad I read this book.

Lyndsey Simpson
Wife and mother

With our feelings and worries so easily all over the place, it is a wonderful thing to read these six expositions of six excellent psalms ('heart songs') and find anchor. William Philip gives such careful attention to God's text and such fitting application to His world that I found myself buoyed up again by the truth and grateful for a small book of pastoral help that I can give anybody and everybody.

Simon Manchester
Former Minister, St Thomas' Anglican Church,
Sydney, Australia

Following a splendid introduction to the Psalter, this marvellous little book exemplifies the very qualities it identifies in the Psalms. As it takes us through Psalms of protest, penitence, pain, promise, pilgrimage and, finally, praise, I found 'my imagination stirred, my emotions excited and my intellect fed.' It is a wonderful blend of raw human experience, intelligent contemporary insight, and good, old-fashioned heart-warming piety. What a lovely book to own, read and give away liberally.

Richard Cunningham
Former Director, Universities and Colleges Christian Fellowship
(UCCF), United Kingdom

Being guided through these ancient Psalms by William Philip is, perhaps unsurprisingly, like watching an experienced physician opening a vintage leather and brass doctor's case only to bring out the very latest cutting-edge diagnostic equipment and treatment. The result is the precise, perfect prescription of remedies targeted with pinpoint accuracy in alleviating the many contemporary spiritual ailments that even mature Christian believers find difficult to shake off. This book is a great encouragement to those who want to engage in real praise of the living God, real prayer to Him, and real preaching of His Word.

What struck me most overall is that he helped me again, to see the complexities of the world in which we live, and the way in which I think, so much more clearly, yet not by looking primarily at either of these, but at the Word of God which so helpfully critiques, and corrects both.

Craig Dyer
Director of Training, Christianity Explore Ministries

HEART SONGS
for
EVERY SAINT

Engaging with God through Times of Darkness and Light

WILLIAM J. U. PHILIP

CHRISTIAN
FOCUS

Scripture quotations are from The Holy Bible, English Standard Version, copyright © 2001 by Crossway Bibles, a publishing ministry of Good News Publishers. Used by permission. All rights reserved. esv Text Edition: 2011.

paperback ISBN 978-1-5271-1136-3
ebook ISBN 978-1-5271-1183-7

Published in 2024 by
Christian Focus Publications Ltd,
Geanies House, Fearn, Ross-shire,
IV20 1TW, Great Britain.
www.christianfocus.com

Cover design by Daniel Van Straaten

Printed and bound by Bell and Bain, Glasgow

For Dick Lucas

With gratitude for a quarter century
of inspiration, encouragement, friendship and love

Your statutes have been my songs
in the house of my sojourning

Psalm 119:54

Contents

When your dwelling is secure
in the LORD's Almighty shadow,
our Refuge, our fortress, the God whom we trust;
from all terrors of the night,
every day's tormenting arrows,
the wings of his truth as a shield hold you fast.

Through darkness we'll walk,
even days of disaster,
before we shall see our true home;
but if thousands may fall,
who know not the Master,
the fate of the wicked he'll keep from his own.

Since you dwell in the Most High,
with my LORD you're bound together,
no plague of dread judgment can darken your home;
for his angels he has charged,
they shall guard your path forever,
borne up on their arms lest your foot strike a stone.

Satan will fall,
though he roar like a lion:
under your feet the Snake slain!
"For you love me" says the LORD,
"your heart is in Zion;
And I will exalt all who honour my name."

"When they call me I will hear:
every cry, and those unspoken,
So shall I be near them, till my Kingdom come;
then deliver them to life,
for my promise stands unbroken,
to share the salvation of Jesus my Son!"

From Psalm 91. Words: WJU Philip; Tune: *Ashokan Farewell* (Jay Ungar)

Preface

This book offers no more than a brief dip into the vast ocean of biblical revelation the Psalms present to us. It is not an attempt at theological study of The Psalms as a coherent book of Scripture (of which there are some fine examples), nor an attempt to expound systematically through any part of it (which many helpful commentaries will do). My aim is much more modest, but, I hope, practical. Looking at a small selection of Psalms – each with a different focus to the Psalmist's prayer, borne out of different experiences in the life of faith – may, I trust, prove fruitful for Christian believers in their own sojourning through life, as they seek to engage with God through times of darkness and of light.

These chapters first found expression in the course of preaching to the fellowship at the Tron Church, Glasgow, at various times between 2008 and 2013. A decade on, I remain thankful for the privilege of serving the Word of God among them.

William J U Philip
July 2023

Introduction

Approaching and using the Psalms

The Psalms are often called the 'hymnbook' of the people of God, and with good reason. As one scholar notes, 'from the earliest times the Psalter has been the Church's manual of Prayer and Praise in its public worship, the treasury of devotion for its individual members in their private communing with God.' Indeed, he can say that 'if a history of the use of the Psalter could be written, it would be a history of the spiritual life of the Church'.[1]

It is vital to note this emphasis on the proper *use* of the Psalms. Many have admired their poetic beauty, enjoying a sense of numinous spiritual 'feeling' in their public expression, whether for example (depending upon cultural background) in the chanting of Coverdale's beautiful words from the Anglican *Book of Common Prayer*, or the evocative metrical psalmody of Scottish traditions. But, though C.S. Lewis is surely right to point out that the Psalms are 'poems, and poems intended to be sung: not doctrinal treatises, nor even sermons',[2] it is equally true that they are not poems written principally for the superficial enjoyment of man. They are written for our serious engagement with God. Psalms are prayers – inspired prayers,

---

1. A.F Kirkpatrick, *The Book of Psalms with introduction and notes: books IV and V* (Cambridge: CUP, 1909), xcviii.

2. C.S. Lewis, *Reflections on the Psalms* (Glasgow: Collins, 1958), 10.

from the Holy Spirit of God Himself – to enable us to pray rightly and truly. As the apostle Paul reminds us, 'we do not know what to pray for as we ought', but, he adds, 'the Spirit himself intercedes for us… according to the will of God.'[3] The Psalms, then, are necessary; gifts of the Spirit, they give us words we can trust and treasure as our own heart songs, as we engage with God through both times of darkness and light in our earthly sojourning of faith. 'We cannot bypass the Psalms. They are God's gift to train us in prayer'.[4]

It is therefore worth drawing attention to some key things we should remember about what they *are*, and what they are *for*, as we think about how to approach and *use* the Psalms.

1. Knowing God – the Psalms teach theology

The Psalms may not be doctrinal treatises or sermons, but they certainly do teach theology. The primary purpose of all Scripture is to bring us to a greater knowledge of God, and the Psalms contain a very profound revelation of God, His nature, and His ways. All the major themes of theology find expression in the Psalms: God's creation, His providential care over the world, man's sin, God's covenant, His instruction (law) and wisdom for human life, His judgment on evil, His way of redemption, and much more. From earliest times, the Church has recognised the Psalter as a microcosm of biblical theology: in the fourth century *Athanasius*, Bishop of Alexandria, called it 'the epitome of the whole Scriptures', and his contemporary, *Basil the Great* of Caesarea, described it as 'a compendium of all divinity; a common store of medicine for the soul; a universal magazine of good doctrines profitable to everyone in all conditions.'[5] *Martin Luther* said the book of Psalms 'could

---

3.   Romans 8:26-7.

4.   Eugene Petersen, *Answering God: learning to pray from the Psalms* (London: Marshall Pickering, 1996), 3.

5.   W. Robert Godfrey, "Ancient Praise," *Reformation and Revival* 4, no.4 (Fall 1995): 61.

well be entitled a "Little Bible" since everything contained in the entire Bible is beautifully and briefly comprehended' therein, and he held that for Christians it 'ought to be precious and dear, were it for nothing else but the clear promise it holds forth respecting Christ's death and resurrection, and its prefiguration of His kingdom.'[6]

This last point is very important indeed, because the Psalms contain a major body of prophetic witness to the person and work of Christ: Jesus Himself says very clearly that they wrote 'about me' and 'must be fulfilled'.[7] While the whole Old Testament anticipates 'the sufferings of Christ and the subsequent glories' of His triumph,[8] it is God's 'anointed one' [His *Messiah*, or *Christ*] – David, king of Israel – whose presence dominates the Psalms.[9] David himself knew that he pointed forward to the coming of great David's *greater* Son, and indeed 'he foresaw and spoke about the resurrection of the Christ'.[10] So it is not too much to say that the Psalms lie at the very heart of the message of the Old Testament revelation of God, the Sovereign LORD, whose everlasting reign is bound jointly with His 'Son', His 'Anointed', His 'King on Zion', the throne of David, forever.[11] It should not surprise us, then, that the Psalms are quoted in the New Testament more than any other book: The New Testament teaches, supremely, about

---

6. Martin Luther, Preface to the Revised Edition of *The German Psalter* (1531).

7. Luke 24:44.

8. 1 Peter 1:11.

9. Israel's kings were known as 'The LORD's anointed One', his *Meshiach*, translated in the Greek OT as *Christos*. See John 1:41.

10. Acts 2:25-31.

11. Psalm 2:2-7. Palmer Robertson comments that we see, particularly in some of the Psalms, 'the certainty of the merger of God's throne with David's throne' and, at the same time, 'the pain, the unending struggle, that will be involved in the full realization of that merger'. O. Palmer Robertson, *The Flow of the Psalms: Discovering Their Structure and Theology* (Phillipsberg: P&R, 2015), 148.

'the kingdom of our Lᴏʀᴅ and of his Christ' who 'shall reign forever and ever'.[12]

2. Knowing ourselves – the Psalms teach anthropology

The Psalms teach profound theology, but they are the antithesis of a dry and rather distant dogmatic tome. There is nothing abstract about any of the theology of the Bible, since in its entirety God's revelation of Himself to human beings is focused on His *relationship* with mankind: created in the beginning, ruptured by sin, but restored to living beauty through the everlasting covenant – promised of old, and fulfilled at last through the Messiah, Jesus Christ. Just as God's law gave instruction for life within that saving covenant relationship established by God's grace, so in the Psalms He has given His people the means to respond relationally to Him: confessing their faith, expressing their love and loyalty, and engaging with Him in the way of most full and wholesome humanity.

The Psalms therefore teach us about *ourselves*, and how we will be most truly *human,* through relating rightly to God in every circumstance of life.[13] In the Psalms 'the Holy Spirit has here drawn to life all the griefs, sorrows, fears, doubts, hopes, cares, perplexities, in short, all the distracting emotions' our minds encounter in life, says John Calvin; thus he was 'accustomed to call this book "An Anatomy of all the Parts of the Soul;" for there is not an emotion of which any one can be conscious that is not here represented as in a mirror'.[14] Athanasius similarly described the Psalms as a *mirror of*

---

12. Revelation 11:15; and ultimately, all his people will reign with him, Revelation 22:5.

13. One of the great existential questions of our age is, what does it really mean to be human?; in that regard, the Psalms have much to teach about where human beings find their true 'identity', and in what true human flourishing really consists.

14. John Calvin, *Commentaries: Joshua and The Psalms* (Grand Rapids: AP&A, 1981), 115-6.

the soul, whereby 'these words become like a mirror to the person singing them, so that he might perceive himself and the emotions of his soul, and thus affected, he might recite them', being led by God-given words to respond rightly to Him in all circumstances, whether seeking repentance, finding reassurance, or expressing praise.[15]

So, the Psalms teach theology in the raw; they touch on every circumstance of real life, and every aspect of humanity – stirring our imaginations, exciting our emotions, as well as feeding our intellects. But they are not like a secular anthropology, teaching about humanity merely in isolation; the Psalms teach a theocentric anthropology – about man in relation to God. And in everything they function so as to address our wills, in order to guide our whole life in relationship with God.

God's revelation is never merely didactic: imparting information. It is always functional:[16] it is His personal word for His people, which both *creates* relationship and *sustains* that relationship. Knowledge of God and relationship with Him go together.[17] In other words, God's revelation is not just to inform us *about* God, but to bring us *to* God, and to go on bringing us closer to Him. A moment's thought helps us understand that language does in fact perform action; words not only say things, they *do* things. When you say to your spouse, 'I love you', you are not merely (or even principally) conveying information, looking for the response, 'that's good!'. No, you are engaging in an action to evoke the reaction:

15. Athanasius, *Athanasius: The Life of Antony and the Letter to Marcellinus*, trans. Robert C. Gregg (Mahwah, New Jersey: Paulist Press, 1980), 111.

16. Isaiah vocalises this infallible, performative aspect which is intrinsic to the Word of God famously when he declares from God 'my word…shall not return to me empty, but it shall *accomplish* that which I purpose, and shall *succeed* in the thing for which I sent it' (Isaiah 55:11).

17. This is something which is witnessed to by the very language of *knowing* in the Bible; the Hebrew word *yada*, 'to know,' itself conveys an intimacy of relationship, such that it is used for the intimacy of the marriage relationship: e.g. 'Adam knew Eve his wife, and she conceived' (Genesis 4:1).

'I love you too' – accompanied by a hearty kiss (and perhaps more)! Likewise, when a couple on their wedding day face each other, and, in answer to the public question in the vows put to them, say 'I do', they are not just saying something, but really are *doing* something very profound: effecting the creation of a lifelong marriage bond. Understanding this helps us to see that we need to think of the Psalms also as functional and performative; we need to ask not just what they teach, but what they *do*: what do the Psalms do *to* us, and *for* us – and what should *we* do with them?

3. Dealing with God – the Psalms help us to pray

The Psalms are not just for knowing God, and knowing ourselves; they are for actually *dealing* with God – for prayer, and for praying. In the Psalms, God has given his people practical tools to *use* in their spiritual lives; as Eugene Petersen has put it, God has given us tools 'for working the faith'.[18]

We recognize that we need and use tools in all aspects of our lives. We have tools for *doing* – cookers, drills, washing machines, laptops etc. – and for *getting* – money, credit cards, shopping trolleys and so on. But Psalms, and the prayers they help us pray, 'are not tools for doing or getting, but for being and becoming.' For being truly human, and becoming *more* truly human – as we learn to deal with God rightly, by answering Him in obedient faith through all circumstances of life – 'for being made into eternal habitations' of the Spirit of God, 'the Psalms are the requisite toolbox…. the best tools available for working the faith.'[19]

The Psalms train us in real prayer, prayer that is honest and comprehensive: not selfish, self-seeking prayer, but rather humble, obedient response to our LORD who has first spoken to us; not blind prayer, 'seeking for God' out there in the dark, as many today seek to indulge the innate human appetite for

---

18.   Petersen, *Answering God*, 2.

19.   Petersen, *Answering God*, 2.

'spirituality'; not prayer to a distant, unknown god we hope somehow to discover through our incantations. The Psalms teach us to pray to the God we know, who speaks our language, and who speaks here to us, teaching us the language of how to answer Him in real faith:

> There is a difference between praying to an unknown God whom we hope to discover in our praying, and praying to a known God, revealed through Israel and in Jesus Christ. In the first we indulge our appetite for religious fulfillment; in the second we practice obedient faith. The first is a lot more fun; the second is a lot more important. What is essential in prayer is not that we learn to express ourselves, but that we learn to answer God. The Psalms show us how to answer.[20]

Prayer is our faith made audible, and the Psalms help anchor our prayer, so that our faith is truly God-centred, focused on humble obedience and service to Him, not mere sentimentality and narcissism. They are a necessary tool to nurture faith so that it does not drift into vague, self-centred spirituality, all about 'expressing ourselves' to God, but rather remains robust and real, upward and outward looking, through real engagement with God in all the changing scenes of our earthly lives.

4. Dealing with ourselves – the Psalms help our praxis

The Psalms are therefore far from theoretical; they are essential guides for Christian *praxis* – that is, the daily, practical exercise of living out our lives of faith. They give us real, 'working models' for living day by day before our Lord, both in our individual lives and also, especially, in our corporate life of worship as we serve God together as His Church.

The Psalms help us deal with all aspects of our sojourning in faith with reality and honesty, offering no escapist fantasies

---

20. Petersen, *Answering God*, 6.

of refuge from life's trials by playing 'let's pretend'. 'Honest emotional struggle stands behind the Psalms';[21] they address every human emotion, giving us both language and form with which to express our passions, our cares and concerns, our thoughts and actions. But they teach us how to handle these rightly: not with repression, which may indeed be harmful, but nevertheless with discipline, doing so in the context of prayer, and of a relationship with God that is 'grounded in our...covenant faith'.[22] The Psalms teach us how to direct our wills, how to behave even in the face of great struggles. Sometimes this is through exhortation: direct commands, such as 'Praise the LORD!' (do it, don't wait until you *feel* like doing it!). Sometimes it is through empathy: more subtly evoking our imaginations, helping us to express questions, fears, even anger, as we pour it out before the LORD. Always, however, the Psalms model for us the way to do this *honestly*, with no pretense; *humbly*, 'I do' not 'I demand'; and *patiently*, with realism about what is 'not yet' in our experience of salvation.

The Psalms really are *working* models to use. It is not just that we learn to pray *like* the Psalms, though that is also true, we are to learn to actually *pray the Psalms*. Hence, by design, the Psalms are timeless; they are a gift to God's people in every place, and in every age. They were prayed not just by the Psalmist, but by his people together as the congregation of the LORD. The Psalms nurtured the faith of Old Testament saints through the ages; they were sung and prayed by Jesus Himself, and by His apostles and they have been used by the Church throughout the millennia since. John Calvin 'expressed the consensus of the praying church when he wrote that the Psalms are "the design of the Holy Spirit... to deliver to the Church a common form of prayer"'.[23]

---

21. Tremper Longman III, *How to Read the Psalms* (Leicester: IVP, 1988), 81.

22. Longman III, *Psalms*, 81.

23. Calvin, comment on Ps. 20:1-2, quoted in Petersen, *Answering God*, 6.

The reason that the Psalms are timeless 'heart songs' for all the people of God, and have instinctively been sung as such by the faithful all through the ages, is because they are the natural songs of all those whose hearts are united forever by faith with Christ, the Anointed King of God. As we have noted, it is David, the LORD's Anointed, who dominates the Psalms, even if not every Psalm is directly ascribed to (or for) him. The Psalms thus breathe the inner life and prayer of the man after God's own heart.[24] In that, as John Calvin rightly says, David represents not only Christ, but also the Church *and* the Christian:

> The personal tribulations of David can give us a foreshadowing *not only* of the passion of *Christ* but *also* of the tribulation which marks the life of the *ordinary Christian* who has to be conformed to Christ. 'David mourns over the injuries which he in particular was suffering yet, in his own person, he represented Christ, *and* the whole body of the Church'.... David is 'the example after which the *whole Church should be conformed*—a point well entitled to our attention in order that each of us may prepare himself for the same condition'....[25]

Christ's prayers, and ours

The Psalms are dominated by 'the prayers of David, the son of Jesse'[26] and there is a clear sense in which David was *not* like us. He was unique, God's Anointed King who, as the leader – and worship leader – of his people, represented and pointed forward to Jesus, the everlasting King, who leads the ultimate song of praise to God 'in the midst of the congregation' of

---

24. 1 Samuel 13:14; Acts 13:32-35.

25. Ronald S. Wallace, *Calvin's Doctrine of the Word and Sacrament* (Edinburgh: Scottish Academic Press, 1995), 49, italics mine.

26. Psalm 72:20.

the redeemed.[27] In *one* sense, therefore, 'all sorts of difficulties with the Psalms are seen to have a solution, when the words are understood to be, first and foremost, the words of Christ our King.'[28]

Nevertheless, as the Psalms themselves bear sharp witness, David himself was very much a sinful human being.[29] He may foreshadow the coming of the last Adam, but he, like us, bears the nature of the first; he was a man of dust, not the man of heaven.[30] David and all the faithful – with him, and after him – were flawed sinners who knew their need, but who experienced God's real grace. They could pray these Psalms truly as *their* prayers, because of the promise of *The* King still to come: because they knew God's wonderful covenant of grace, and because they had faith and trust in the LORD. The Spirit of God thus moved *them*, in these *former* days, to pray these prayers of true faith; yet their prayers 'written in former days' were 'written for *our* instruction' in the Church of Jesus Christ today.[31] And how much more may we, living now in these *last* days, pray such prayers – as the Spirit of the risen, glorified humanity of the LORD Jesus bears witness deep within our spirits that we are children of God, having open access to our Father![32]

---

27. Hebrews 2:12.

28. Christopher Ash, *Teaching Psalms Volume 2: From text to message* (Fearn, Ross-shire: Christian Focus, 2018), 26.

29. See, for example, Psalm 51.

30. 1 Corinthians 15:45-48.

31. Romans 15:4.

32. The language used in Hebrews, of how 'much more' glorious and excellent the blessings of fulfilment in the New Covenant times are than in the age of promise does not denigrate the reality of Old Testament faith and experience; rather it magnifies the blessings of our New Testament experience as even 'better' than something already wonderful. OT believers prayed the Psalms, truly engaging with God in a real way as their own experience of real, living faith was forged throughout their lives. How much more is our privilege of access to God, having all that they had, and so *much more* (See Hebrews 3:3; 8:6; 9:14; 12:9).

True believers, whether of former days, like the prophets and psalmists, or of these latter days in which we live, are servants of the LORD whose lives are united to their Saviour King, and therefore whose prayers, also, are united to His. The Psalms are *our* prayers also; as Augustine put it, 'we recite this prayer of the Psalm in Him, and He recites it in us.'[33]

Prayer and praise amid darkness and light

Christ the Saviour who prayed the Psalms was, however, like David, a king whose earthly path was marked by much tribulation, suffering, and hatred. That is why we find, in reading the Psalms, that so many of them (over half) are *laments*: sad songs, expressing torment, brokenness, suffering and, very frequently, the attack of enemies. So, if it is true that the Psalms are purposed by the Holy Spirit as a common form of praise and prayer for the Christian church, then we must ask ourselves whether the contemporary church pays enough attention to this, both in the expectations we have of the path of 'normal' Christian experience, and also how this is expressed in the kind of songs we sing and prayers we pray, both individually and together.

Perhaps we may harbour some sense of guilt: that, living as we do in these days of fulfilment, however we might feel, our praise must always sound more jubilant even than the most exultant praise of, say, the final Psalms of the Psalter (Psalms 145-150) – for don't we exult in a *risen* LORD, and proclaim the triumph of His victory? Indeed we do; we are an Easter people, and Hallelujah is our song. However, as C.S. Lewis reminds us,

> Christians know something the Jews did not know about what "it cost to redeem their souls". Our life as Christians begins by being baptised into a *death*; our

---

33. Augustine, *Enarratio in Psalm 85*, quoted in Petersen, *Answering God*, 4.

most joyous festivals begin with, and centre upon, the broken body and shed blood. There is thus *a tragic depth in our worship* which [the Old Testament faith] lacked. *Our joy has to be the sort of joy which can coexist with that*; there is for us a spiritual counterpoint where they had simple melody.'[34]

Christ's people are called to walk joyfully *with* Him; but His way is the way of the cross, and our joy must be the sort of joy that can coexist with this. Our prayers of praise, exulting in God's promises, must likewise be the kind of prayers that coexist with prayers of penitence, those expressing, at times, loud protest, and sometimes voicing deep and dreadful pain. We shall find that, as we recite the prayer of the Psalms in Him, and He recites them in us, they will become our true heart songs throughout our earthly sojourning as saints in Christ Jesus, leading us along the path of healthy faith and trust as we engage with our God, both through times of darkness and light.

---

34. C. S. Lewis, *Psalms*, 48 (italics mine)

When God Seems Absent

Psalm 10 – a song of protest

[1] Why, O LORD, do you stand far away?
   Why do you hide yourself in times of trouble?

[2] In arrogance the wicked hotly pursue the poor;
   let them be caught in the schemes that they
   have devised.
[3] For the wicked boasts of the desires of his soul,
   and the one greedy for gain curses and renounces
   the LORD.
[4] In the pride of his face the wicked does not seek him;
   all his thoughts are, "There is no God."
[5] His ways prosper at all times;
   your judgments are on high, out of his sight;
   as for all his foes, he puffs at them.
[6] He says in his heart, "I shall not be moved;
   throughout all generations I shall not meet adversity."
[7] His mouth is filled with cursing and deceit
and oppression;
   under his tongue are mischief and iniquity.
[8] He sits in ambush in the villages;
   in hiding places he murders the innocent.
 His eyes stealthily watch for the helpless;
[9]   he lurks in ambush like a lion in his thicket;

he lurks that he may seize the poor;
   he seizes the poor when he draws him into his net.
10 The helpless are crushed, sink down,
   and fall by his might.
11 He says in his heart, "God has forgotten,
   he has hidden his face, he will never see it."

12 Arise, O Lord; O God, lift up your hand;
   forget not the afflicted.
13 Why does the wicked renounce God
   and say in his heart, "You will not call to account"?
14 But you do see, for you note mischief and vexation,
   that you may take it into your hands;
  to you the helpless commits himself;
   you have been the helper of the fatherless.
15 Break the arm of the wicked and evildoer;
   call his wickedness to account till you find none.

16 The Lord is king forever and ever;
   the nations perish from his land.
17 O Lord, you hear the desire of the afflicted;
   you will strengthen their heart; you will incline
   your ear
18 to do justice to the fatherless and the oppressed,
   so that man who is of the earth may strike terror
   no more.

Psalm 10

In recent years Britain has been shocked by multiple trials and convictions of large 'grooming' gangs for the most appalling acts of depravity in sexually abusing and prostituting young children. In one such case the judge said that these men put the girls through 'a living hell' and reading just some of the press reports revealed why: the sheer, callous wickedness was indeed hellish. But perhaps the most scandalous aspect of many of these cases was that though the police had been involved on many occasions over several years, questioning many of these men after multiple complaints were made, nothing had been done to put a stop to these terrible crimes. It was strongly suspected that because these gangs were almost exclusively young, Muslim men of Pakistani origin, the authorities were too fearful of the charge of 'racism' and 'islamophobia' to risk 'community upset' by doing more. So the wicked, shameful exploitation went on for years and years. It is no surprise that there were many howls of protest. The responsible Chief Constable in one case was grilled by John Humphrys on Radio 4's *Today* Programme, who put it to her that, given the Force's knowledge of the evil but their abject failure to intervene – which allowed that evil to go unchecked – the Police, and indeed the Chief of Police, were surely culpable. 'Should you not resign?' he said to her; understandably, there were many similar calls.

In the same way, many questions have been asked of those in positions of power and authority in the BBC during the 1970s and 1980s as it has emerged there was a widespread culture of star presenters sexually abusing women and even young girls in a carefree way. Those in high places in the BBC, we now know, knew what men like Jimmy Saville and Stuart Hall (and who knows how many others) were doing. But it seems they did not use their authority to stop, nor even to censure, the perpetrators. So is it any wonder that people should now protest, and do so very strongly, as the ghastly realities have become public?

Likewise there were many protests in the public square in the wake of the global financial crisis about government regulators of the financial services industry, and the chiefs of the big banks on whose watch, and through whose reckless negligence, huge losses resulted. While vast numbers of people suffered the fallout of the economic collapse their actions caused, huge burdens of debt and taxation were placed on populations, and ordinary people saw their savings capacity obliterated through near-zero interest rates (one of the most effective wealth transfers from the prudent to the prodigal in history). Many of the elites waltzed off into the sunset with bonuses and pensions most people could only dream of.

Our world is full of loud and bitter *protest* at these, and many other, terrible injustices. When power and authority has failed, where there has been dereliction in duty, it is quite natural for people to protest.

Give up on God?

What about when the One in ultimate authority, who has supreme power, seems to be in dereliction of duty: should we not protest? Should we not call for *His* resignation? When we look around at our world and we see it full of wickedness and evil, with so much injustice and apparent failure to hold perpetrators to account, should we not call for *God's* resignation? Shouldn't we show *God* the door? Is it not time to give up on God and put our trust elsewhere: in another religion, another philosophy, another spirituality – in something or someone that will deliver better results for our lives here on planet earth?

Many people *have* done that in protest at what they perceive God has done – or more often *not* done – in their own personal lives. Usually it is when something touches life close to home that this happens; headlines that may unsettle us when they are at arm's length out in the world can utterly devastate us when they invade our own lives. So often it is when personally touched by loss, bereavement, or tragedy of some kind that people say, 'That is it; I've had it with God! It is time for you to resign, God; in fact I'm sacking you. Get out, I want nothing more to do with you in my life!'

The Psalmist here in Psalm 10 is not quite saying that, but it *is* a real song of *protest* – at the apparent silence and absence of God, and at His seeming failure to use His power and His authority to do what He ought to do. *Why?* That is the question at the beginning of this Psalm: 'Explain yourself to us, God, because surely you have some explaining to do.'

¹ Why, O Lᴏʀᴅ, do you stand far away?
   Why do you hide yourself in times of trouble?

This is a question I am sure most of us will have asked God at one time or another, and what this Psalm teaches us is that such protest to God is not always wrong; indeed, it tells us it is an integral part of the life of faith. Real, biblical faith does not, ever, hide away from the truth; it is all about facing up to reality in this world, because it seeks a divine explanation of that reality. So the Psalmist is not showing God the door, as it were; he is interrogating God. He wants answers, and he won't let Him go until he gets them. So, if we look closely at this Psalm of protest about God's apparent absence in the face of evil that is rampant in the world, we will learn from the Psalmist's faith-provoked, and ultimately faith-strengthening, interrogation of the Lᴏʀᴅ. His honest, but anguished, heart song to God falls into three parts: first, a real protest, a real problem, and a real prayer.

A Real Protest

The Psalm begins very abruptly, and somewhat shockingly, with words of real protest at the apparent *absence of God*: 'Why, O Lᴏʀᴅ, do you stand far away? Why do you hide yourself in times of trouble?' (1). Why are you hiding, God, when surely you should be acting – *intervening* against evil and for good? 'In arrogance the wicked hotly pursue the poor; let them be caught in the schemes that they have devised' (2).

What are you waiting for, Lᴏʀᴅ? It is an agonised cry of protest and it stems from a sense of a perplexity about God seeming to be acting in such an un-Godlike way. Where is the God who is sovereign and is good and who works justice? Most Bibles say in a footnote that Psalms 9-10 belong together as companion pieces and in the Greek Old Testament they appear joined as one Psalm.[1] (This is probably why Psalm 10 has no title like the others around it; the title of Psalm 9 covers both). The context of Psalm 9 makes this protesting question of 10:1 even more understandable. Verse 4 of Psalm 9 reminds us that God is a God of *just judgment*: 'for you have maintained my just cause; you have sat on the throne, giving righteous judgment.' Verse 6 speaks of enemies being rebuked and rooted out. Verse 8 is utterly clear: 'He judges the world with righteousness.' It goes on relentlessly: 'The wicked shall return to Sheol [to death], all the nations that forget God' (17). But this is not what the Psalmist seems to be seeing: not now, not even most of the time!

When there is a clear disjunction between our credo – what we believe about God – and the observable facts in our lives and experience, it is understandable that we have doubts. We believe that God *is* just and good, and that He *is* ultimately powerful, on the throne of the whole universe. But when we see with our own eyes many things that suggest that He does not intervene when He could, or that He is not intervening when He *should*, then we are bound to ask why – 'Why not? And why not *now*, Lord? Why do you stand far off?'

That protest is real, and it is one we often make in our own prayers. Sometimes it expresses doubts of an intellectual kind – perhaps we are wrestling with issues of science, for example. But most often I think the doubts which make us protest to God the most are about suffering, especially unjust suffering, and, above all, when these things come up close and personal, to affect us in our own lives. We probably do not like to admit it, but usually we are only bothered in a rather abstract, intellectual sort of way by innocent suffering in the world; we become bothered in a much more passionate and visceral way when we see ourselves as the innocent victim. That is when we really start to protest!

---

1. Taken together, Psalms 9-10 make up a single acrostic, that is, each stanza beginning with a successive letter of the Hebrew alphabet.

But is it wrong to protest – like verses 1 and 2 of this Psalm?

No – because here it is in our Bibles, as a Psalm that is preserved to be sung by the LORD's people; we are even given its choral instructions in the superscription to Psalm 9. So, here is a song of unashamed protest given to God's people, not to be hidden away as if it was somehow unworthy, but right here in the congregational hymnbook of Israel. Indeed, as we look through the Psalms, many of the sung prayers of God's people are full of questions, doubts, perplexities, and protest to God. Indeed, the very last words of prayer we hear from the lips of the LORD Jesus echo the Psalmist's frequent protest: 'My God, why have you forsaken me?'[2] He is asked the oft-repeated question: 'Why do you hide yourself in times of trouble?'

Doubts and protests like this are not a manifestation of unbelief, of abandoning faith. They are the very opposite; they spring *from* faith. The protest here is not *rejecting* God; The Psalmist is remonstrating *with* God. He is calling Him by name: 'Why, O LORD' – 'O *Yahweh*' – the personal name of the God he knows.[3] That is the whole point. The sharpness of the problem for the Psalmist is because he *knows* this God: he knows what He is like, he knows His goodness, he knows His grace, he knows His righteousness, and he knows His justice. That's what makes the situation so very painful, because it seems his God is not being true to His own character.

That is why the Psalmist is protesting so seriously, just as you or I would do if we had a close friend we know and love, but who seems to be acting totally out of character: doing wrong, being negligent, acting in a way that is utterly beneath themselves. We would not be dispassionate about that with a

---

2. Psalm 22:1; Matthew 27:46.

3. Most English Bibles translate as LORD in capital letters the Hebrew letters YHWH, which is the revealed covenant name of the God of Israel (See Exodus 3:13-16). Pious Jews considered the name too holy to be spoken aloud, and so when reading the Scriptures they would substitute 'Adonai' – 'My LORD' for every instance of YHWH; hence the custom still in many Bible translations is to render it LORD. Some older translations use a vocalized version of the Hebrew, "Jehovah", although more likely the pronunciation should be 'Yahweh'.

friend, or with one of our children. We remonstrate with them, we confront them, we protest: 'That is not who you are!' And of course, the closer that relationship, the more passionate the protest is going to be: 'This just isn't *you*! What is going *on* with you? Why are you acting like this? Don't *be* like this!'

This is the issue for the Psalmist, as it is for us so very often when we find ourselves questioning God. As Ralph Davis puts it, 'This is not merely some intellectual quandary but a devotional dilemma.'[4] The Psalmist cannot understand what the LORD is doing, or rather why He is not doing what he feels He ought to be doing. Yet he is still dealing with the LORD; he hasn't rejected Him. He is wrestling *with* God, and that is a sign of real faith.

If you find yourself in that place at the moment, perhaps feeling that your prayers to God are much more full of protest than of praise, do not despair. Don't doubt the reality of your own faith because you find yourself full of doubts and questioning about God. These struggles, even these real protests, are the hallmark of both real faith and *realistic* prayer. You are in good company when you find yourself with these sort of questions on your lips, crying out, 'Why, O LORD?'. It is a genuine question, found throughout Scripture, which involves grappling with the mystery of the apparent absence of God in the face of evil, and especially in the face of unjust suffering.

The answer never comes by trying to close our eyes to all the difficulties that confront our faith, but rather in facing these facts squarely and honestly. We must not try to close our minds protectively, as if hiding from reality would somehow preserve our faith. There is no integrity in that – and no protection in it either. If our faith cannot stand up to hard scrutiny of the reality of life, then surely it will wither and die in the end, because it won't be real, but a false trust. No; far better a faith

---

4. Dale Ralph Davis, *The Way of the Righteous in the Muck of Life* (Fearn, Ross-shire: Christian Focus, 2010), 118.

that confronts reality and does not try to bury reality under pious platitudes. Far better a real *protest* at the apparent absence of God than an unreal *pretense* that just tries to hide it all away, because in the real world we cannot avoid real problems.

A Real Problem

The problem to be faced up to in verses 2-11 is the unaccountability and sheer *arrogance of the godless*. We have already acknowledged the general problem of evil and the apparent absence of God, but here in the Psalm it is not so much so-called 'acts of God' in view, but the acts of man. It is not the problem of tsunamis, earthquakes, and other tragedies that kill innocent people, but the acute moral problem of human arrogance and wickedness that troubles the Psalmist: 'In arrogance the wicked hotly pursue the poor' (2), 'the wicked boasts' in his greedy exploitation (3) feeling unassailable, 'in the pride of his face' cursing any thought of judgment, or even divine presence (4).

In the Bible 'the poor' are not just the economically poor, but all those who lack power, lack control, or are helpless under the influence of others. The word 'helpless' occurs repeatedly in the Psalm (8, 10, 14) and it is these hapless, helpless and wretched souls who are 'crushed', and 'sink down' under the hand of the wicked (10). That is a huge moral problem, and one that troubles every decent human being. We must remember that morality is not just the prerogative of Christian people. Sometimes Christians talk as though the rest of the world were always immoral or amoral, but that is foolish, and people get rightly annoyed when they hear that sort of thing. It is simply not true that only the religious have a developed sense of morality. Of course we, as Christians, would want to point out respectfully that we believe the origin of that morality does indeed come from God, that it is part of the innate reality of being human, because we are creatures made in the image of God. Although that image is fallen, and far from perfect

due to our sinful natures, God's image remains nevertheless –
however unconscious a person might be of that fact. So by their
very nature they have a sense of what is right and wrong, what
is just and unjust, however imperfect their conscience might
be.[5] This is a vestige of the rightness of God that is imprinted
upon the human mind. We know what is fair and unfair; that
is why some of the very first words that children ever speak are
'that is not fair!' And we keep on saying words like that all of
our life: 'where is justice in this world of ours?'

Of course the logical answer of those who take refuge in
the reductionist worldview of atheistic Scientism today is that
there is none, and can be none. Might is right; it is the power
of our selfish genes that is in charge, according to Richard
Dawkins, for example. It can sound so plausible, so scientific
and impressive, when you read his books (and he is a fine
writer). But when you translate these ideas into the realm of
real life, they just do not give satisfactory answers to the moral
problems of our universe. There are real problems which cannot
just be explained away by evolutionary biology or anything
else the merely physical sciences can teach us. If the selfish
gene really is the driving force of this universe, if we are just
dancing to the music of our DNA, if there is no evil and no
good, if there is just blind pitiless indifference in the universe,
as Dr. Dawkins maintains[6] – then why should we feel horror
at the sex-slave gangs, the people smugglers, the abusers of the
helpless who have made fortunes for themselves and enriched
their lives by their 'trade'? Should we not rather applaud them
for the triumph of their self-serving *achievement* all these years?
That just is not how real people think, is it? – unless they are
sick and disturbed, people who should be in prison or in secure

---

5. Though sin causes people to 'suppress the truth', they cannot completely
suppress the knowledge of God, hence there is no excuse for immorality
(Rom. 1:18-20); the human conscience still 'bears witness' to the law of God
(Rom. 2:15).

6. Richard Dawkins, *River Out of Eden: A Darwinian View of Life* (New
York: Basic Books, 1995), 133.

hospitals. No. Decent people rightly have a sense of moral outrage at such things. Moreover, if justice is not done, then it is a huge problem.

But here is the issue: if that is so for every decent person in this world, then how much bigger is that problem for the Christian believer who, like the Psalmist, worships the God of Psalm 9:8 – who is a righteous Judge, who we believe 'judges the world in righteousness' and 'judges the peoples with uprightness'? How much bigger is that problem for us, when *we* see such moral outrage so close at hand – and God apparently doing nothing about it?

Wickedness up close

This Psalm certainly has the feel of first-hand experience, and there is nothing that can sensitise us to the outrage of theft or violent assault or murder or rape nearly so much as when it comes close to home and affects us personally: when it is *your* house burgled; when *your* son has been beaten to a pulp, or *your* daughter raped or murdered; when it is *your* livelihood ruined through someone else's wrongdoing.

Verses 3-11 describe such wickedness seen up close, and it is the world all of us recognize so clearly. The Psalmist lays out the character, the conduct, and the credo of the wicked man for, ultimately, what he believes drives what he is and what he does.

The character of the wicked

Verses 3-6 display a character full of an arrogant invincibility: in his arrogance (2) he boasts and curses God (3); he 'puffs' at his foes (5); he says 'I shall not be moved' (6) – in other words, 'I'm invincible'. I remember once speaking to a young man who had been a soldier serving in Afghanistan. He said when he came home from there his mother had lost weight and looked gaunt; she hadn't been sleeping, worried sick the whole time that he was there. No wonder! Which mother wouldn't feel that way with her son in harm's way? But he said, 'The strange thing was that *I* felt utterly invincible, that nothing was ever going to happen to me'. That is the reckless audacity of the young soldier, and the wicked man here has that same sense of invincibility.

The conduct of the wicked

Verses 7-10 demonstrate his conduct is that of very active iniquity: his mouth and tongue deceive and oppress, serving himself and destroying others (7); his eyes are on the main chance to prey on the helpless (8b-9); his hand is quick to violence and murder, profiting from the misfortune of the poor (8a,9). Think of the loan shark roaming the housing estate, or the drug pusher, and the control they exert over the hapless who have fallen into misery. At the other end of the scale, think of the Bernie Madoffs and others who defraud thousands of the wealthy of their money with their Ponzi schemes – and everything in between. This is the world as we know it, and it is all because so many say in their heart, '"God has forgotten, he has hidden his face, he will never see it"' (11). There'll be no reckoning; God is dead, or He does not exist, or if He does exist He is impotent. He'll never judge. He'll certainly never judge *me*.

The credo of the wicked

It is this credo of practical atheism which drives the evil that issues from the heart of man. Whether we really deny God's existence intellectually or whether just in practice, that is the way so many people think: 'it'll be OK in the end with the Big Man upstairs.' How many times have you heard that sort of thing expressed? Human beings have changed God into a creature of our own making, to serve us the way we want Him to. And, of course, we very much prefer a god who is blind, a god who suffers from amnesia, and a god who will never ever judge anybody – least of all me.

Sadly, that attitude is almost as common today inside the professing church as outside. But we should know that this is not new either, because the Psalmist here is describing what he sees *inside* the community of faith, among those who, at least outwardly, profess to be the people of the LORD. Yet they are arrogantly assured of their own invincibility and of God's impotence to do anything in the face of their sin. I think perhaps one of the most striking incidences of that attitude I have ever witnessed was once at a denominational gathering where an ordained minister stood proudly regaling all with stories of his sexual lifestyle, utterly at odds with the Word of God, and then sneered mockingly as he said, 'and not one church roof has yet fallen on my head and brought judgment down upon me. Ha-ha-ha!'; 'There is no God' to judge; 'he has hidden his face, he will never see it'; 'I shall not be moved.' That is the confident boast of the ungodly, and so often it seems to be that 'His ways prosper at all times' (5).

That is a real problem, and the Psalmist does not hide it. Indeed quite the opposite. As Derek Kidner says, he touches 'the nerve of this problem' to 'keep its pain alive, against the comfort of our familiarity, or indeed complicity, with a corrupt world.'[7]

The Bible honestly confronts reality and the problem of evil. Far from allowing us to anaesthetize ourselves, it drives us to confront this truth and also to confront greater truths that alone will keep us from despair and disillusion about this world. He reminds us that there is evil in the heart of man and that that is not just *a* problem but in fact it is *the* problem of this world. This is what the whole biblical gospel is about: bringing an ultimate answer to all such evil through the coming of God's everlasting kingdom. It is grappling with *that* reality that drives the Psalmist to real prayer.

---

7. Derek Kidner, *Psalms 1-72: An Introduction and Commentary* (London: IVP, 1973), 71.

A Real Prayer

The prayer of verses 12-18 is a real prayer, prayer rooted in the *assurance of the gospel*. The protest of real faith gives way to the prayer of real faith for the coming of the kingdom of God according to promise, as God shows Himself not to be absent, but active *amid* much apparent darkness, and true to who He really is: the righteous one who will set *all* things *right*, according to His promise and according to His plan.

Arise, O God

There is a noticeable change in tone at verse 12; the Psalmist prays now with a real sense of hope, 'Arise, O Lord; O God, lift up your hand.' There is a confidence in God, and a clear sense that the self-confident assurance of the wicked is greatly misplaced, despite all of his boasts.

The Psalmist's protest now is levelled squarely at the wicked man in verse 13: 'Why does the wicked renounce God and say in his heart, "You will not call to account"?' Not so, says the Psalmist. It is not that he is disregarding the reality of evil and its oppressiveness in this world; he has been absolutely honest about that. Rather, as Derek Kidner says, he is speaking 'in faith *about* faith'.[8] That is, he is saying that this is not the only truth to be considered here; there is more. No longer is he viewing things merely from below, with the narrow-focused lens of mere earthly sight. He is panning out so that his visual field is wider and higher: so that he sees more, and greater, truth from above. He is looking to what he knows to be equally true, both in his own experience and through God's revelation in Scripture: that God is never absent, even when He may seem to be. Rather He is active, but He is working according to His own perfect timetable and His own perfect plans. He *will* show Himself to be the God who is just and good and powerful and true. God does *see* (14); He is *sovereign*, 'king forever and ever'

---

8. Kidner, *Psalms 1-72*, 71.

(16); and He will *save*. He will 'do justice to… the oppressed' and likewise destroy those who terrorize them now, so that they 'may strike terror no more' (18).

It is because the Psalmist knows all *these* things are *also* true that he can pray as confidently as he does in verse 15, for God to 'break the arm of the wicked', that is, to break the power of evil and to call to account all that is wrong at the bar of divine justice.

What a difference this perspective on the totality of the situation makes! Knowing this reality means the believer – who often *is otherwise* 'helpless' (14) – can gladly abandon himself to the LORD, in the face of much perplexity and doubt.[9] The reality of a troubled world hasn't changed. It is still there; he hasn't pretended it away. But knowing something crucial about the bigger picture of that reality *has* changed everything about how he faces up to the world.

Seeing the bigger picture

What a difference seeing and understanding the bigger picture makes, especially in a war against evil. In 1940, during some of the darkest days of World War 2, Britain was facing massive aerial assault from the Luftwaffe. Fearful observers on the ground were often found asking, 'where on earth are the RAF?' as Nazi bombers and fighters came relentlessly across the Channel in vast numbers, apparently unopposed. The view from the cockpit of those bombers was correspondingly triumphant; it seemed to be that there were no British fighters to come up and challenge them. Many of the coastal towns were badly bombed and suffered because of that lacking counter-attack. But what those on the ground, and those in the invading cockpits, did not know, was that the RAF was not absent. The secret advances that the British had made in radar

---

9. The verb *azab*, translated 'commit' in verse 14 more usually means abandon, forsake, leave; c.f. Psalm 16:10 'For you will not *abandon* my soul to Sheol'.

technology meant that the invaders' every move was being watched, and charted across all the chain of home stations linked around the coast. So only when the enemy bombers came close enough inland – where fighter planes could come back down to refuel at RAF home bases, and where British pilots who were shot down could parachute to safety and go straight back up in other planes – was the command given for the defending planes to go up. Wave after wave of surprise attacks then come upon the enemy, who had been lulled into a false sense of security; what seemed like an indestructible force that would destroy this nation and pave the way to all-out invasion was in the end repulsed and destroyed.

How different reality looked if you knew not only the view from the ground but also the view on those radar screens in the home stations. Well, verse 14 tells us that God in heaven *does* 'see' and 'note' all the evil and the wickedness in this world and in men's hearts, and He *will* take it in hand.

Seen by a higher power

Some years ago when I was living and working in London, I had to attend what was euphemistically known as a Speed Workshop. I had been travelling up to a conference in Northamptonshire and taking a speaker to that conference. We were deep in conversation (about the interpretation of prophecy!) and, no doubt distracted, driving through one of the little villages I got caught by one of those nasty speed cameras hidden behind a bush. I was doing 37 mph in a 30 mph zone, and so a letter came offering me the choice: three points on my licence and a £60 fine, *or* paying £60 for the privilege of going to a Speed Workshop! (but avoiding the three points on my licence). I chose the latter option – but not without a lot of self-righteous grumbling![10] That day of the Speed workshop turned out to be something of a disaster. I had to drive all the

---

10. I recommend the avoidance of millennial discussions while driving – and probably at all times, for that matter!

way from south London to Northampton, to spend the whole day, which was bad enough. But when I got there I found I'd forgotten my wallet, so I couldn't buy any lunch, but then, even worse, I nearly ran out of petrol on the M25. I had to phone a friend in north London and go and borrow £10 from her to get enough fuel to see me back home. But, in a strange way, the Speed Workshop itself was a very useful experience (apart from the £60!). They told us all sorts of things about where you would find speed cameras and what triggered them. I am not sure if they were really intending to help us to get around the speed traps or to encourage us not to speed, but I certainly got better at spotting them from then on!

However, there is one thing from that day that I will never forget. They showed us photographs of various speeding incidents, and one was footage of a motorbike rider speeding through a little village every morning to his work. He went through the speed camera every single day at 110 mph in a 30 mph zone! Now a motorbike has no number plate on the front, and since the speed camera's view was only looking at the speeding motorbike from the front, he was never being caught. He clearly knew this; they showed us picture after picture every day from the camera with the motorbike rider speeding past defiantly, making obscene gestures at the camera!

But *then* they showed us two more pictures taken on one day, seconds apart. One was the rider going through at 110 mph and making an obscene gesture at the camera. What he did not know, however, was that the county council also had *mobile* speed cameras, and that on this day right around the corner from that fixed camera, was a mobile camera which took his photo from *behind*. The next picture showed him clocked at 110 mph with his rear number plate plainly in view. A final picture was the report from the local newspaper of his conviction: an enormous fine, loss of his licence, and imprisonment.

'But you do see'...

...you will incline your ear

to do justice to the fatherless and the oppressed, so that
man who is of the earth may strike terror no more.

(Ps. 10:14, 17-18)

Shocking, and Saving, Sovereignty

Those who think God is blind, and does not see, and won't
ever call to account are in for an almighty shock – far greater
than the shock that biker got. Because God *does* see. He sees,
and He records, all wickedness and arrogant pride in the
human heart. What a shock it will be to the nations that He
is sovereign, the King forever and ever, and that He will save
those who abandon themselves to Him, bringing justice to
the fatherless and the oppressed. The rude reality is that those
who think they are invincible are not immortal, but, as verse
18 says, they are just creatures 'of the earth', who return to dust
to 'strike terror no more'. One day they *will* face the terror of
Him who 'calls wickedness to account *until he finds none*' (15);
that is, God will pursue just retribution to the very last detail.

The Psalmist's prayer in verse 12 is rooted in the assurance
of the gospel, that, as the whole Bible teaches, God is not
absent, even if He may appear to be. He is active: He *has* arisen
and taken the whole problem of evil in His hand. The whole
story of the Bible is how He is bringing verse 18 to its final
consummation: in a relentless, inexorable way He is constantly
at work doing this, however absent He may sometimes seem
to be to His children.

This is His pattern. Think of Joseph, and how God was
not absent, but active, even amid all the evil that surrounded
his life, to work a great salvation.[11] Think of the Exodus,
when God's people Israel were crying out believing God had
abandoned them, and yet already His deliverer Moses had been
born, who would lead them to rescue from the Egyptians.
And never forget the greatest darkness of all, the darkness of

---

11.   Genesis 37-50, whose story is summed up famously in Genesis 50:20,
'you meant evil…but God meant it for good'.

Calvary, when surely the faithful lamented, and protested to God, 'Why does He not save Jesus from the cross?', and even the Son of God Himself lamented in prayer, 'Why?'. 'My God, why have you forsaken me?' It was this same song of – ultimate – protest: 'Why do you hide yourself in times of trouble?'

But in the darkness God was not absent. He was active: arising, lifting up His hand to remember His afflicted ones, to bring righteousness to His own, and to destroy – forever – the terror of His people.

So don't panic when evil abounds, and it seems God is absent, uncaring, or impotent. Whether it is physical persecution against believers, as in many places today, or corruption in the professing church, or the ferocity of temptation of the evil one in your own heart: Don't panic. Don't try and pretend these things away either; you can't, they are all too real, and it does no good at all to try to hide from reality.

Rather, let your protests to God lead you to real prayer to God – prayer rooted in the assurance of His gospel: of the God who does see, and who is sovereign, and who will save according to His certain promise and plan. And as you do that, as verse 17 says, He will strengthen your heart, and will go on strengthening it every day until that great day when His judgment is no longer hidden, but fills the earth with His justice.

Right Sacrifices from Real Sinners

Psalm 51 – a song of penitence

To the choirmaster. A Psalm of David, when Nathan the prophet went to him, after he had gone in to Bathsheba.

¹ Have mercy on me, O God,
according to your steadfast love;
according to your abundant mercy
blot out my transgressions.
² Wash me thoroughly from my iniquity,
and cleanse me from my sin!

³ For I know my transgressions,
and my sin is ever before me.
⁴ Against you, you only, have I sinned
and done what is evil in your sight,
so that you may be justified in your words
and blameless in your judgment.
⁵ Behold, I was brought forth in iniquity,
and in sin did my mother conceive me.
⁶ Behold, you delight in truth in the inward being,
and you teach me wisdom in the secret heart.

[7] Purge me with hyssop, and I shall be clean;
    wash me, and I shall be whiter than snow.
[8] Let me hear joy and gladness;
    let the bones that you have broken rejoice.
[9] Hide your face from my sins,
    and blot out all my iniquities.
[10] Create in me a clean heart, O God,
    and renew a right spirit within me.
[11] Cast me not away from your presence,
    and take not your Holy Spirit from me.
[12] Restore to me the joy of your salvation,
   and uphold me with a willing spirit.

[13] Then I will teach transgressors your ways,
    and sinners will return to you.
[14] Deliver me from bloodguiltiness, O God,
    O God of my salvation,
    and my tongue will sing aloud
    of your righteousness.
[15] O Lord, open my lips,
    and my mouth will declare your praise.
[16] For you will not delight in sacrifice, or I would give it;
    you will not be pleased with a burnt offering.
[17] The sacrifices of God are a broken spirit;
    a broken and contrite heart, O God,
    you will not despise.

[18] Do good to Zion in your good pleasure;
    build up the walls of Jerusalem;
[19] then will you delight in right sacrifices,
    in burnt offerings and whole burnt offerings;
    then bulls will be offered on your altar.

Psalm 51

The answer to the first question of the *Westminster Shorter Catechism* about the purpose of humanity's existence declares that 'man's chief end is to glorify God and enjoy him forever'. If that is so, then we must understand *how* we are to glorify God – how we are to offer God true worship – in every part of our lives, and in all circumstances, including the very dark ones we find ourselves in through our own fallenness .

Our word 'worship' derives from the old English word meaning worth-ship, ascribing, showing, and displaying worth. True worship means expressing the true 'worth-ship' of God: giving God His rightful worth above everything else in our lives. The New Testament makes very clear that nothing is more important in life; the chief calling of all of our lives as Christian people, according to Peter, is to live so that 'in everything God may be glorified through Jesus Christ', because 'to him belong glory and dominion forever and ever.' (1 Pet. 4:11). In *all* of life we are to offer up our bodies, as living sacrifices, 'holy and acceptable to God', says Paul; this is what constitutes our 'spiritual worship' (Rom. 12:1). We are to *continually* offer up sacrifices of praise to God, says Hebrews 13:15, 'the fruit of lips that acknowledge his name'.

But what does that really mean? How are we to be true worshippers or, in the words of this Psalm (51:19), how are we to offer 'right sacrifices' that delight the LORD our God? And above all, *how do we do that when we have made a real mess of things:* when we are feeling guilty, because we *are* very guilty, and because we know we are. Perhaps we may have fallen into some very specific sin, some very bad behaviour we have been part of, and we know it. Or maybe we have become entangled in a pattern of habit that has a hold on us, which we know is damaging and destructive, and we know is displeasing to God. Or maybe we have just realised that we have drifted a long way spiritually: we have cooled off, sliding back a long, long way from being the keen Christian that we once were.

What is the answer to that problem? What is the answer that will get us back to a better place spiritually? How are we to offer 'right sacrifices' then?

Getting back on track with God

Often the answer that you find from spiritual refreshment books, or a conference you might go to, is a call to re-dedication to Christ, an act of decisive re-consecration and commitment. That might mean a renewal of effort and devotion, a pledge of a new discipline in prayer and Bible reading perhaps, maybe even a defined set of steps that take you on the path back to holiness – a decisive offering to God of a renewed sacrifice of praise in your life.

But supposing part of that new discipline in prayer and Bible reading takes you to Psalm 51; it might prove to be rather disconcerting. Verse 16 poses something of a problem to that whole approach to getting ourselves 'back on track' to the right place with God: 'For you [God] will *not* delight in sacrifice… you will *not* be pleased with… offering.' It seems God is not interested in what we can bring Him by way of some kind of special spiritual exercises! The sacrifices *He* is interested in are described in verse 17 as the deep matters of the heart. It is not what we *bring* but what we must *be*: having 'a broken and contrite heart, O God, you will not despise'.

Now that is a real problem, because it does not describe the natural human heart. Nor, if we are honest, does it describe the Christian believer's natural heart condition either; the beauty of the meekness and humility it speaks of is the very opposite of what we know very often to be the truth about our own hearts. These are characteristics that cannot be produced by ourselves; they are things that *happen* to our heart. Our heart must *be* broken, it must be *made* contrite, literally crushed, by somebody else. We cannot simply manufacture this by our own spiritual exercises or disciplines; that is just not possible. So then, must we despair?

No. This Psalm is here because David wants to teach fellow sinners to learn what he learned: that it is God alone who can make real worshippers of us, and that He can do so, and does do so, *even* when we find ourselves in the most dreadful mess of our own sin; even when we find ourselves in the midst of a disaster of our own making. David wants to teach fellow 'transgressors' like us *God's* ways of making us broken and contrite in heart, so that – even though we are still real sinners – we 'will return' to God (13) and we *can* make right sacrifices which will again delight the heart of our Father in Heaven. And His wonderful message is that, even though we may have been paralysed by shame and guilt and despair, we can come rejoicing again to the LORD because, in His great mercy, He will rejoice again and delight in us.

Psalm 51 is perhaps the best known of all the so-called Penitential Psalms, prayers of confession, expressing profound penitence of heart in the face of the recognition of human sinfulness.[1] And what it teaches us is that what we need, when we are in a terrible mess of guilt and sin – and shame and despair – is not a fresh personal *discipline* in *our* work for God; rather, what we need more than anything else is a fresh personal *discovery* of *God's* word to us, and of His work *for* us and *in* us through His covenant of abundant mercy and steadfast love.

That is what David discovered and that is what this Psalm wants us to discover also: that it is God's word of revelation which does God's work of renewal, and which leads us to His witness of righteousness in us, and through us to the world. It is the gospel alone, when it invades our hearts personally and powerfully, that can elicit right sacrifices from real sinners. Psalm 51 teaches us how that happens.

The Word of God's Revelation

It begins by giving testimony to David's great discovery in the word of God's revelation. The gospel brings the word of God's

---

1. Seven Psalms are traditionally grouped together as penitential: Psalms 6, 32, 38, 51, 102, 130, and 143. There are well-known musical settings of many of these, particularly dating from the Renaissance period, including settings of all seven by Orlande de Lassus, and William Byrd. Individually, Gregorio Allegri's setting of the *Miserere* (Ps. 51) is most famous.

revelation to us and, as we shall see, it is a revelation of horror
and yet also hope.

The first words of the Psalm are the superscription and
they tell us when the Psalm was written, on the occasion when
Nathan, the prophet of God, went to David after he had gone
in to Bathsheba.[2] If you do not know the story, read it first in
2 Samuel 11-12. It's a sad, shocking story about Israel's greatest
leader falling onto a disastrous conveyor belt of sin, which went
from lust, to adultery, to cover-ups, even to murder – and then
all hushed up, as though life could go on as normal after all of
that. *But*, says the last verse of that story, 'the thing that David
had done displeased the LORD' (2 Sam. 11:27).

We need not dwell on the particularities of David's crimes
here, because there is a danger that in doing that we miss the
point entirely. We might think, 'That really *is* shocking and
thank God I've never committed adultery or at least never
murdered anybody to cover it up.' But that is absolutely not the
point. The point is quite the reverse: that if David – the great
leader *par excellence* of God's people, God's anointed king, a
man after God's heart who walked in His ways like no other
– can sin so badly and have to confess his sins in the manner
of this Psalm, then how could any of us think that we would
never be capable of these kinds of transgressions? This Psalm
reminds us that no one, not even the most revered Christian
leader, is exempt from learning these lessons. I was reminded
of that as I worked on this chapter: I was reading words written
on this Psalm by someone who was once looked up to as a fine
preacher and Christian leader, but who fell into a disaster not
unlike David's, and, to my knowledge, has not repented. It was
chilling to think that the writer probably would not want to
even read those words now, far less write them himself.

But in His great mercy, God was not silent and did not
abandon David. The word of His revelation came to him

---

2. The superscription in our English Bibles constitute verses 1-2 in the
Hebrew Text; verse 3-21 in Hebrew correspond to v1-19 in English Bibles.

through the prophet Nathan in a powerful way (1 Sam. 12:1-7). He first outraged David by telling him a parable about a man who had done great wickedness, so that David in the end cried out, 'In God's name, this man deserves to die.' And then came Nathan's rapier thrust: 'You are the man!' And in a split second, everything that David knew about God, and about himself before God, suddenly became acutely and overwhelmingly true to him personally. He was undone; God's revelation came like a hammer blow to David. And the whole of this Psalm expresses what God revealed to him in that encounter. 'You are the man!'; it took just a few words to thrust it home. Think of Peter when the cock crew; for him it required not even words, just the crow of a cock, but it brought right home to his heart everything Jesus had said about him in an instant. He knew that it was true and all his own words of bravado were shown to be utterly false (Mark 14:72).

Sometimes that is all it takes in our experience too: just a few words, and like a great thunderclap God's Word is like a hammer that cracks open our heart.[3] Perhaps it is a scornful challenge to you from somebody at work: 'You're not one of those *evangelical* Christians, are you?' 'No', you say because you do not want to be mocked – and like Peter, you are suddenly hit in the pit of your stomach. You are exposed, just as David was, to a revelation of real horror, as you are brought abruptly face to face with the truth about your own heart.

A Revelation of Horror

That is what David is giving voice to in this Psalm, in verses 2-6; the word of God's revelation has revealed to him the *absolute corruption of his character*. So often it takes an experience like this to expose the truth we have been hiding from.

Sin anaesthetizes us and makes us deceive ourselves. We know that we do wrong but, of course, we make excuses so easily. We say things like, 'I know I'm not perfect but...'

---

3. Jeremiah 23:29.

meaning, 'Well I'm not *that* bad, really'. We do it when we apologize, because more often than not we do not actually apologize. We say, 'I'm sorry *if* I've upset you, *but...*' What we really mean is, 'It is your fault for being upset, not mine.' Or we say, 'Yes, I'm sorry but, you know, I'm very stressed', or 'you have to understand my background, I can't really help it', or 'I was just born like this, it is in my genes', or 'with all the pressure of society today, with the media and so on ...' In other words, anybody else is to blame except *me*! Or perhaps we do it more subtly: outwardly saying the opposite, blaming ourselves all the time. 'Oh it's my fault, I'm so, so bad!' But, deep down, we know that if we say that sort of thing it prompts somebody else to say, 'No, no, it's *not* your fault. Don't beat yourself up'. Instead of justifying yourself, you get somebody else to justify you, and so you can absolve yourself of responsibility for your wrongdoing. The ways that the human heart can find to minimize and mitigate our sense of sinfulness are absolutely legion, and of course they are given plenty of help today by psychologists and sociologists and other 'ologists' galore.

But God's word of revelation cuts right through all of that and it faces us with the truth, and the truth is an X-rated picture of real horror. That is the picture David has been forced to view, and he describes here for us. It is not that he is just describing for us one particular action. Rather, it is this action, now met with God's penetrating revelation, which has torn his heart open and shone a bright beam to show what is in his heart *all the time*, and has always been there. If your church uses a projector, imagine if during a service there appeared on the screens not the Sunday notices, but all the secrets of *your* heart – the hidden deeds, words and, worst of all, thoughts – of which you would be most ashamed. Just thinking about that makes the colour drain from my face. But that is what it feels like, when God exposes us by His Word, up close and personal.

That was certainly David's experience. He had to face the fact that his sin was not an uncharacteristic lapse. It was not a slip-up, so that he could say, 'That is not really me at all.'

No, his sin was profound and perverse and pervasive. Even worse, it was deeply personal; it was a scandalous affront to God Himself.

The grim truth about our sin

Suddenly, all the teaching that he knew in his Bible about sin came right home to his own heart in that deeply personal way. He uses all the great words the Bible uses for wrongdoing here. 'Cleanse me from my *sin*' (2), 'My *sin* is ever before me' (3). That word means a falling utterly short in every possible way, missing by a mile what he ought to be as a true human being. He is full of *iniquity* (2), a *perverse* twistedness in his character, which is *pervasive* from before even his birth: 'In sin did my mother conceive me' (5). He is not saying his birth was illegitimate or that sex is sinful, but rather that sin is utterly basic to his personhood, that it is woven into every single part of his whole life and history, and always has been. His sin is also *profound:* where God delights in truth deep in 'the inward being', he knows that his 'secret heart' is absolutely rotten to the core (6). Above all, and worst of all, it is deeply *personal*: 'transgression' means sinful and wilful rebellion against God Himself: 'Against you, you only, have I sinned and done what is evil in your sight' (4).

Do you see what a horrible, horrific revelation this is for David to come to terms with? He is seeing himself – the true David as he really is – and he cannot deny the absolute corruption of his character. His crime was 'no freak event: it was in his character; an extreme expression of the warped creature he had always been'.[4] And he must acknowledge the truth of God as it comes home, deeply and painfully, to his 'secret heart' (6).

It is a common thing, when someone has been arrested for an awful crime, for a friend or a relative interviewed on the TV to say, 'I know it must be a mistake because I know him and he

---

4. Kidner, *Psalms 1-72, 190.*

is just *not capable* of doing such a thing.' Sadly, such sentiments betray naïveté about the human heart; none of us will ever believe, on our own, what we are really capable of doing and being. But God's Word reveals that truth to us, exposing the awful truth about our hearts – very often when we have said or done something wrong, and we cannot hide from that horror. We cannot gainsay the fact that our 'heart is deceitful above all things', that it is 'desperately sick', as Jeremiah the prophet reminds us (Jer. 17:9).

Learning the truth about our own hearts, coming to terms with the absolute corruption that is in our own character: that is the very first lesson in the class of worship 101. Without that there can be no hope, none at all, of restoration to God. Jesus makes exactly this point in a story He told in Luke chapter 18: two men went into the temple to pray. One was a Pharisee, a very upright man, and the other an absolutely rotten tax collector; but he was the one who knew his own heart. He was the one who beat his breast and said, 'Be merciful to me, a sinner.' And Jesus said it was he, and not the other, who went home 'justified' – right with God.[5] That is because it is only when we have been left reeling by this revelation of real *horror* about our own heart that our eyes are opened and our ears sensitized to a revelation of real *hope* – in the truth about *God's* heart, and in His absolute commitment to His covenant.

A Revelation of Hope

What possible hope can there be for us in the face of a horrific realization about the pervasiveness and the permanence of sin and evil in our hearts? Surely if we have begun to be honest with ourselves, we must know that God knows and we cannot deceive Him. How can He possibly forgive me yet again? On what basis can I even *ask* God to have mercy upon me yet again?

---

5. Luke 18:14.

The answer lies in verse 1 of the Psalm: 'Have mercy on me, O God, according to your *steadfast love*; according to your abundant mercy.' The same authoritative revelation that exposes our absolute corruption reminds us of God's *absolute commitment to His covenant.*

God's 'steadfast love', His *hesed*, is His unfailing covenant love and loyalty, and the whole story of the Bible is about that utter commitment to His people. It's a story of repeated tragedies, in the sin of His people, and the repeated triumphs of God's grace. From Genesis onwards, the dramatic family sagas of Abraham and Isaac, and the tumultuous unfolding story of Jacob and his twelve sons, preach the same message – He will not let His people go. His *hesed*, His covenant loyalty, His steadfast love, is utterly tenacious, and His abundant mercy is utterly tender and compassionate. We see so vividly this divine mercy and compassion reflected in the life of Joseph, the LORD's servant, and saviour of his family, when *his* compassion welled up in his heart for his brothers, despite all that they had done to him, and he had to run out of the room and weep, so tender was his mercy towards them (Gen. 43:30).

The greater truth about our salvation

The same revelation from God, which came home to David's heart waking him up to the horror of his sin, also awakened him to the great hope in the LORD's covenant mercy. That is why I think Myles Coverdale's version of this Psalm in the English *Book of Common Prayer* is right to translate verses 7 and 8 as indicative rather than imperative mood (as statement of fact rather than a command or request):

'You *shall* purge me with hyssop, and I shall be clean;
    you *shall* wash me, and I shall be whiter than snow.

> You *shall* make me hear joy and gladness
>   that the bones you have broken may rejoice.' [6]

David had a promise of God's mercy in the Scriptures. The very chapters in Moses' Law that gave him these words to describe his own sin, also showed him the way of cleansing promised through the washing and purging of God's appointed sacrifice.[7] That is why he had hope – in the midst of horrible and horrific honest truth about his own sinful heart. It is a wonderful mystery of God's providence that what man means for evil, God Himself intends for good. Even here, through David's manifest evil and sin, he comes nevertheless to not only a greater knowledge of himself and his own sin but a greater knowledge of the love and the mercy of his covenant God. Sometimes the same is true for us also: out of a pit of our own making our eyes are lifted up to God – because we have nowhere else to look – and we see a new vision of the wonderful covenant mercy of God in the gospel of Christ.

If that covenant mercy blessed David's heart with a wonderful hope in the midst of the misery of his sin – if the sprinkled blood of bulls and goats of the sacrifices gave him a wonderful assurance of real cleansing from God – then the New Testament says to us *how much more* does the blood of Christ purify *our* consciences (Heb. 9:14)! How much *more* do we, who have the fullness of the revelation of the cleansing blood of the everlasting covenant, know that abundant mercy and steadfast love of our God!

---

6. 'Thou shalt purge me with hyssop, and I shall be clean : thou shalt wash me, and I shall be whiter than snow. Thou shalt make me hear of joy and gladness : that the bones which thou hast broken may rejoice.' The Psalter, *Book of Common Prayer*, 1662.

7. Read Leviticus 14 and Numbers 19 for references to 'washing', which was ceremonial cleansing (not actual bodily washing) through sprinkling of water from hyssop twigs; how much more the ultimate washing is fulfilled by the sprinkled blood of Christ (Heb. 9:13-14; 20-22; 10:22), signified in the sprinkled water of Christian baptism (1 Pet.3:21-22).

We have so much more than even David had. Every time we sit around the LORD's Table, we are calling God to remembrance of His absolute commitment to His covenant, and in faith crying out 'you *shall* wash me, and I shall be whiter than snow' based upon His steadfast love, His abundant mercy sealed forever unbreakably, and unshakeably, in the blood that was poured out at Calvary. The gospel word of God's revelation that has filled us with horror about our complete sinfulness fills us all the more with a hope of our complete salvation.

The Work of God's Renewal

It is not just a future hope that the Psalmist speaks of. It is clear that the word of God's revelation is bringing about the work of renewal in David's life, as it does in our lives as we respond in trusting faith to that word. It is the gospel that does God's work of renewal in us, and that renewal is marked both by the humbling of true repentance and also by the healing of true relationship.

The humbling of true repentance

It is David's grasp of the gospel that draws out his response in confession in verse 1. It is always God's revelation that elicits from our hearts a right response towards God. That's what the Bible means when it speaks about *faith*: the rightful response of humble obedience to God's Word to us in the gospel. David is convicted; he is full of a godly sorrow, the godly grief that leads to the humbling of real repentance 'that leads to salvation' (2 Cor. 7:10).

David is full of grief for sin, and desire for real restoration. The knowledge of sin *and* the knowledge of God's grace is what moves him to seek that grace – 'blot out… wash me… cleanse me'. It is a *sovereign* grace that he is seeking, with real and true heart humility. He is absolutely clear that all of this is something that only God can do – *he* can do nothing. That is so clear in verses 9-12. Only God can blot out his iniquities; God must hide His face from his sin and turn aside His personal wrath and anger. Only God can 'create… a clean heart' (10). That word 'create' is only ever used in the Bible when speaking of God; it is the word from Genesis 1 when God created out of nothing the whole world, and it is God alone who must create a wholly new heart in David. David is praying for a miracle – *he* cannot do it, God must do it because *only* God can *renew* him and make him new. There is no hint anywhere of him saying something like, 'All right, LORD, please forgive my lapses. I promise I'll atone for my sins, I promise I'll turn over a new leaf.' That is not what he is praying – not at all! It is the opposite of that. Real repentance is marked by the utter humbling that says,

> 'Nothing in my hand I bring, only to your cross I cling, stained by sin to you I cry, wash me, Saviour, or I die.' [8]

God's renewal always humbles us, with a humbling that characterizes all true repentance.

The healing of true relationship.

His gospel also heals; it heals the broken relationship that lies at the very heart of the tragedy of sin. It heals and restores our joy in the LORD and our knowledge of the LORD Himself.

Verse 11 shows us that David's greatest fear is for what the guilt of his sin will do to his experience of the presence of God:

> Cast me not away from *your* presence,
> and take not *your* Holy Spirit from me.

He feared, no doubt, what happened to Saul. Saul was chosen by God, and was anointed as king; but Saul was rejected by God because of his sin and rebellion against God, and we are told that God removed His Spirit from him (1 Sam. 16:14). But David's very desire for the joy of the LORD – for the presence

---

8. from the hymn *Rock of Ages*, by Augustus Toplady.

of the LORD – is the evidence that God *has* renewed a willing spirit within him. It is evidence that God has *not* abandoned him. His tears and his fears are the testimony to the healing of reconciliation, not the hardening of rejection. The difference between David and Saul is the same as the difference between Peter and Judas. Both sinned – both denied and betrayed their LORD; but where Judas went out and hanged himself, with the worldly grief that only produces death (Matt. 27:3-5), Peter wept bitterly (Matt. 26:74-75), and that was a godly grief that led to salvation, like with David here.[9]

This is something so important to distinguish, and so important for us to know. Sometimes Christians can be so filled with shame at their sin, they become overcome with fear and anxiety that they have sinned fatally against the Holy Spirit; they believe that they may have committed the unpardonable sin Jesus speaks of, so they think 'God must have taken His Spirit from me and I'm lost.'[10] But that cannot be so; the tears, and their fears of that, are the very evidence that it is not so! They are the evidence that there is an on-going relationship with the LORD Himself, a desire in the heart which is alive for the presence of God, a yearning for the joy of His salvation. That is the godly grief that leads to repentance and restoration, not a worldly grief that leads to death. The one from whom God's Spirit really has withdrawn has no such fears and no such tears: no sign of humility and penitence, just haughtiness and pride, the very opposite.

But where the gospel is bringing the word of sovereign revelation, God's Spirit is at work, bringing about a work of sovereign renewal to His people. He humbles them in true repentance and heals them, and restores true relationship – with God Himself, and therefore also with all God's people who, together, will rejoice in the love and the mercy of a covenant God like this. This is what brings about, and restores,

---

9. 2 Corinthians 7:10.

10. Matthew 12:31.

true *worship* and will result in the 'right sacrifices' (19) from sinful people, 'a sacrifice of praise to God, that is, the fruit of lips that acknowledge his name' – lips that are opened by God to declare the praise of the God of steadfast love, the God of abundant mercy.[11] This is what is so evident in the final verses of Psalm 51.

The Witness to God's Righteousness

Verses 13-19 are all about the Psalmist's lips being opened by God's restoring grace and now bearing witness to His righteousness. It's the gospel that brings the word of God's revelation *to* sinners, and the gospel that does the work of God's renewal *in* sinners; so also it is the gospel that draws out the witness to God's righteousness *from* sinners – as that righteousness is declared to the world, and demonstrated in His people. '*Then* I will teach transgressors [fellow sinners] your ways' (13, emphasis added); '*Then* my tongue will sing aloud of your righteousness... my mouth will declare your praise' (14, emphasis added).

'The saddest thing about sin in the believer is that it closes his mouth and negates his testimony.'[12] We could say exactly the same about the church as a whole. When the Spirit of the LORD is grieved away because of unrepented sin, where there is pride instead of penitence, where there is hiding of sin and even laughter at sin instead of horror at sin, then no amount of 'offerings and sacrifices' can possibly compensate.[13] There will

---

11. Hebrews 13:15.

12. James Philip, *Psalms: Reading the Bible with James Philip* (Glasgow: Tron Media, 2014). James Philip's Bible Readings (on Psalms and all other Bible Books) are all available for free at the Tron Church website. https://www.tron.church/resources.

13. 'What to me is the multitude of your sacrifices? says the LORD; I have had enough of burnt offerings...' was God's verdict on unrepentant Israel, who did grieve his glory away from his own Temple, and themselves into Exile, where at last they learned, bitterly, the real sacrifices of broken hearts (Isa.1:11; c.f. Jer. 7). My colleague Bob Fyall has suggested it is possible verses 18-19 were added to Psalm 51 during the Exile by part of the faithful remnant, realising

be no living and powerful witness to the glory of God from such a people; no amount of 'religion' can ever build up the church or impact the world. The sacrifices God wants are not pathetic manifestations of empty ritual. He wants powerful manifestations of His righteousness alive in His people.

Such real praise that sings aloud God's righteousness to the world comes where sinners know the truth about themselves and their sin, when they have been faced with the horror of it – its depth, its pervasiveness, its perversity – and have been floored by that. Real praise like this comes when people know that horror, and yet have tasted, again and again, the joy and hope of a gospel of abundant mercy and steadfast love – that there is grace abundant to cover all their sin, that there is grace to create and renew a clean heart within them, and that there is grace to restore the joy of the Lord's saving presence! Then, and only then, will there be powerful praise – powerful witness, personal and public – to the righteousness of God through His redeemed people. *Then* there will be the right sacrifices that the Lord delights in (19): the fruit of lips, and of lives, that truly confess His name, His greatness, His goodness, and His grace. *Then* God's *righteousness* – His saving mercy in the gospel of our Lord Jesus Christ – will be declared in the world's hearing from tongues that 'will sing aloud of your righteousness' (14).

A Revelation of Righteousness

You cannot suppress the joyful testimony of a sinner truly forgiven and made new in the Lord Jesus Christ! Nor can you hide the witness of a church where true gospel revelation is working true gospel renewal. The gospel works throughout the assembly, deep in people's hearts: slaying pride and conceit, humbling them all in true and real repentance, uniting all, and healing and restoring relationships broken by sin,

---

that David's experience had become their own. Certainly these prayers would have a deep poignancy for those longing for restoration, and knowing now, beyond all pretension, that they were dependent wholly on the grace and mercy of God to sinners.

and thus demonstrating God's saving righteousness in living human hearts.

When the people of this world encounter a community like *that* – men and women deeply conscious of the abundant horror of their sin, but also deeply conscious, and deeply thankful, for the super-abundant mercy of God in Christ – *then* they will see that they are not encountering vain and empty religion and ritual; they will see that they are encountering the power and the beauty of the God who washes the filthy until they are whiter than snow, the God who makes them dance for joy because of His saving righteousness.

That is why this Psalm ends in verse 18-19 with a prayer for Zion, for the whole of God's city and His people – which in these last days means for us the whole Church of the Lord Jesus Christ. Through Him we too can pray with the Psalmist:

> 'Do good' to her; "build up her walls" – through this gospel of abundant mercy.'

> 'May the word of your great *revelation* do your work of great *renewal*, so that all your people will witness to your great *righteousness* – so that sinners, like us, will return to you, and transgressors may know your marvellous ways.'

These signs of the living work of the Spirit of Christ spilling out from among His people, the fruit of lips that acknowledge His name, are the 'sacrifices' and 'burnt offerings' and 'whole burnt offerings' that the Lord delights in.[14] And so surely this is a prayer that we will all want to echo for our own lives, and also for our churches: that we, who know we are great sinners, will find ourselves leading other great sinners, to our great Saviour.

---

14. Verse 19; Hebrews 13:15.

When We in Darkness Walk

Psalm 88 – a song of pain

A Song. A Psalm of the Sons of Korah. To the choirmaster: according to Mahalath Leannoth. A Maskil of Heman the Ezrahite.

[1] O LORD, God of my salvation;
    I cry out day and night before you.
[2] Let my prayer come before you;
    incline your ear to my cry!

[3] For my soul is full of troubles,
    and my life draws near to Sheol.
[4] I am counted among those who go down to the pit;
    I am a man who has no strength,
[5] like one set loose among the dead,
    like the slain that lie in the grave,
  like those whom you remember no more,
    for they are cut off from your hand.
[6] You have put me in the depths of the pit,
    in the regions dark and deep.
[7] Your wrath lies heavy upon me,
    and you overwhelm me with all your waves. *Selah*

[8] You have caused my companions to shun me;

you have made me a horror to them.
I am shut in so that I cannot escape;
9   my eye grows dim through sorrow.
Every day I call upon you, O LORD;
    I spread out my hands to you.
¹⁰ Do you work wonders for the dead?
    Do the departed rise up to praise you? *Selah*
¹¹ Is your steadfast love declared in the grave,
    or your faithfulness in Abaddon?
¹² Are your wonders known in the darkness,
    or your righteousness in the land of forgetfulness?

¹³ But I, O LORD, cry to you;
    in the morning my prayer comes before you.
¹⁴ O LORD, why do you cast my soul away?
    Why do you hide your face from me?
¹⁵ Afflicted and close to death from my youth up,
    I suffer your terrors; I am helpless.
¹⁶ Your wrath has swept over me;
    your dreadful assaults destroy me.
¹⁷ They surround me like a flood all day long;
    they close in on me together.
¹⁸ You have caused my beloved and my friend to shun me;
    my companions have become darkness.

Psalm 88

When we are full of the joys of answered prayer, it is easy to sing – and good to do so. But what about when our prayers are apparently not being answered or – worse – when our experience echoes Job's when he cried to God for help:

'But when I hoped for good, evil came,
    and when I waited for light, darkness came'

(Job 30:26)

What songs do we want to sing then – if we can bear the thought of singing at all – when the answer coming from God Himself seems to be not good, but evil- not light, but darkness?

I will never forget the funeral of a friend just a little older than myself, a strong Christian believer and longstanding leader in his church. He had suffered a terrible period of very severe depression requiring him to be hospitalized, and while in hospital, he took his own life. He left a wife and son, and a daughter due to be married just a few weeks later; it was heartbreaking. What songs could my friend have sung in the tortured darkness of the misery that led him in the end, in the confused agony of his condition, to take his own life? And what could his grieving family sing to express the heartbreak and the trauma that looks into the future with nothing but bleak and barren bereavement? Not long afterwards, a close friend in ministry called me to say that one of his oldest friends, a Christian man who had mentored him in the faith since his teens, had been found, having hanged himself. He also had descended into a darkness of desolation, and his death likewise left many others groping in anguished sorrow and grief – my friend included.

Songs for our misery

What songs can a Christian believer sing when their only experience seems to be one of evil and darkness? When tragedy strikes and strikes again, in a sudden grief or sickness or relentless sorrow of some other kind? *What do miserable Christians sing?*

That was the title of an article in a theological journal some years ago.[1] Commenting on the fact that the Psalms are so rarely sung in contemporary evangelical churches, the author, Carl Trueman, suggested that the reason is because so many

---

1. Carl Trueman, "What Do Miserable Christians Sing?" *Themelios* 25, no. 2 (February 2000): 1-3. Available at https://www.thegospelcoalition.org/themelios/article/what-do-miserable-christians-sing/.

Psalms are taken up with lamentation: with feeling sad and unhappy and tormented and broken. We in the West, however, live in a culture that wants to hide away from these things, and in the church the tendency is to do the same. And so, he says, a 'diet of unremittingly jolly hymns inevitably creates an unrealistic horizon of expectation which sees the normative Christian life as one long triumphalist street party'.[2]

Not only is this quite wrong theologically, it is disastrous and cruel pastorally. The truth is that we do live in a world of broken people, where tragedy and sorrow are real and are present, sometimes in an overwhelming way. To deny that, and to force people to pretend – to hide away their sorrows, to keep their pain cloaked in a mantle of superficial piety – is not only to sin against the *truth* of God, but to sin grievously against the *child* of God who is suffering so bitterly in the darkness. So what *do* we sing and pray 'when we in darkness walk, nor feel the heavenly flame?'[3] One powerful answer is that in giving us 'the Psalms God has given the church a language which allows it to express even the deepest agonies of the human soul in the context of worship'.[4]

Psalm 88 is one such Psalm. Derek Kidner says, 'there is no sadder prayer in the Psalter' and surely that is so.[5] Unlike many Psalms – which, like Psalm 40, begin in the miry pit and end with the God of deliverance – Psalm 88 begins with the 'God of my salvation' but it ends only in utter 'darkness'. There is no light, no dawn to lift the gloom; there is only unremitting despair in this prayer. And yet here it is in the Psalter, as part of the corporate worship of God's Church. Notice the title, it is a song to be *sung*: written 'to the choirmaster' with instructions

---

2. Trueman, "Miserable Christians", 2.

3. From the Hymn 'Your Harps ye trembling saints', Augustus M Toplady (1740-78).

4. Trueman, "Miserable Christians", 2.

5. Derek Kidner, *Psalms 73-150: An Introduction and Commentary* (London: IVP, 1975), 316.

probably about the tune and how to sing it.[6] This is not a prayer to be hidden away in embarrassment; it is a prayer needed by the Church of God, and it comes from the pen of a very well-known man, 'Heman the Ezrahite'. He was one of 'The Sons of Korah', pioneers and leaders of song that David set up in Israel, a man renowned for wisdom; indeed, perhaps only Solomon was wiser.[7] Among others, he was in charge of all the song for the temple of the LORD.[8] The Sons of Korah were responsible for some of the richest Psalms in the Psalter, some of the most joyful praise, as you will see if you look back to Psalms 84 and 85.

But here is a Psalm, from this man of great gifts and renowned spiritual wisdom, full of deep and dreadful darkness. It is no accident that we have it in our Bibles; it is the provision of the compassion and mercy of our God, a God who knows our frame, who remembers that we are dust and who bears us gently in His hands in all our darkness, our sorrows and our despair. For such times He has given us this deeply painful prayer, for a deeply pastoral purpose.

A Deeply Painful Prayer

This Psalm expresses the honest response of a godly, mature believer to deeply painful darkness. Structured as it is around three heartfelt cries to God – 'O LORD, God of my salvation, I cry out day and night before you' (1); 'Every day I call upon you, O LORD' (9); 'But I, O LORD, cry to you' (13) – Alec Motyer summarises these as describing *life without light*, *death without hope*, and *question without answer*.[9]

---

6. 'according to Mahalath Leannoth' is likely a tune, and 'A Maskil' the nature of the verse.

7. 1 Kings 4:31.

8. 1 Chronicles 6:31-3.

9. Alec Motyer, "Psalms," in *The New Bible Commentary 21ˢᵗ Century Edition* (Leicester: IVP, 1994), 543.

A cry of agony

The first outpouring of this deeply painful prayer in verses 1-9 is a cry of deep agony – agony which expresses the deep darkness of a life that is totally devoid of light. He is living, but it is a living death.

Verse 6 encapsulates the experience: 'You have put me in the depths of the pit, in the regions dark and deep'. That language of 'the deep' is very significant in the Bible, beyond even the obvious allusions of darkness we instinctively understand. The opening lines of Genesis 1 speak of chaos and void, when darkness was over the face of 'the deep' – the place of primeval terror before God said, 'Let there be light'. This is the place of utter darkness; it is the place devoid of any life at all. It was these 'fountains of the great deep' which were opened once again in Noah's day to engulf all of life, bringing darkness and death again over the earth.[10] It is this overwhelming darkness that has engulfed the Psalmist.

He is still alive: there is still day and night (1) during which his relentless cries are ringing out. Yet his day has been turned into night. He lives constantly in deep darkness, and all the usual comforts of the night – sleep and refreshment – have leached away into sleepless agonies. He cannot sleep; he tosses and turns, crying out to God, but his words are unheard and unheeded. It is as if God is not there – as if he is living in another world, a world of the dead where no one hears him.

Living death

Physically he fears he is near death: 'my life draws near to Sheol' (3), the place of the dead. Some scholars think that he is describing leprosy, and verse 5 describes life in a leper colony, a grim place where the 'living dead' lived apart, shunned and stigmatised. That is possible, but we must remember this is poetry, and the language ought not to be taken too woodenly.

---

10.   Genesis 7:11.

Verse 3 is speaking about more than *physical* life ebbing away. 'My *soul* is full of troubles' he says, the Hebrew word indicating the whole person. It is as though he is saying 'my whole being, to its very core, is deeply troubled'. He is expressing the deep melancholy someone can feel even if they are not physically ill or suffering from some terminal affliction. They can feel as if all their strength is being sapped (4); they can feel utterly cut off from normal life (5); they can feel like theirs is truly a living death in an agony of darkness (6).

Depressive illness is a scourge of our modern Western world, and anyone who has any experience of this will well recognize the Psalmist's words here. But severe grief, especially if the bereavement has been particularly tragic, can also plunge people into 'regions dark and deep' (6) such that it, too, feels like a living death. People use exactly that language: 'a part of me died when my beloved wife died', 'a part of us died when we lost our child.' You have likely heard people say such things, and perhaps you have said it yourself. Sometimes, stress becomes so great as to feel simply overwhelming, so that someone feels they are drowning. That is the language of verse 7, which speaks of being overwhelmed by the waves. Many things in life can make people feel this way, and again it is exactly the language we use: 'It's all getting on top of me', 'I feel overwhelmed', 'I can't keep my head above water, I'm drowning!' 'I'm "in the depths" in a dark pit of chaos that I cannot escape' (6). It is a *living death*: all the normal joys of life are gone. Even natural appetites for food and for sleep have shrivelled up. The Psalmist gives voice to the dreadful sense of isolation these feelings bring: shunned by his friends, 'shut in' upon himself, in desolating loneliness, with a sense of total rejection by everyone (8).

That isolation can be real, of course. People are generally not good at knowing how to relate to someone who is suffering great pain like that, whether it is suffering due to grave depression, or grief, or loss. We tend to back off, not knowing what to say, and that can lead to real isolation. But often it is just imagined, part of the distorted view of reality of this condition. Sometimes an experience of pain or loss causes past hurts in our lives that have been long buried to rise up to the surface, and we project all of those feelings onto present relationships, believing ourselves to be rejected and scorned and looked down on by everyone. These experiences can bring an overwhelming sense of darkness into life so that it really feels like the light of life has been totally snuffed out, as though you will never escape from the depths of a deep, dark pit.

This gifted, deeply respected, mature, wise believer, Heman, felt just like this. Furthermore, just *because* he was a man of faith, he felt it even more keenly and with even greater agony. In verse 7 there is a clear sense of something even more terrible than his present earthly darkness: it is the terrifying horror of what you might call a heavenly darkness – 'Your wrath lies heavy upon me'. It is his knowledge of this eternal dimension that brings the deepest agony of all.

A cry of anxiety

That is what the Psalmist articulates in his second cry in verses 9-12, a cry of dreadful anxiety – anxiety which expresses the dread darkness of death under God's wrath. He is living with the fear of looming damnation.

'Is your steadfast love declared in the grave... or your righteousness in the land of forgetfulness' (11-12)? His fear is of death looming, with no assurance of eternity, no assurance of an ongoing relationship with the LORD, no salvation from the God of his salvation. His fear is death with God's wrath still heavy upon him, and therefore that he will soon be beyond the place of salvation, beyond His righteousness, beyond His covenant love and faithfulness, beyond His saving wonders. We must not misunderstand this. Heman is not articulating here the supposed ignorance of Old Testament believers who knew nothing about life beyond the grave, assuming that hope is only for this life and death means the end of everything. His point here is precisely the reverse: Like Hebrews, he believes that 'it is appointed for man to die once, and after that comes judgment', and it is precisely this judgment he fears because he thinks he is still under God's wrath.[11] The Psalmist, like other Old Testament saints, knew that well. The Psalter opens with a Psalm contrasting the ultimate future of the wicked, who will not stand in the ultimate judgment, and the righteous, who will.[12] Psalm 49, another of the Psalms of the Sons of Korah (perhaps also written by Heman, among others), likewise clearly describes this judgment of the godless, and the divergence for those who trust in God:

> Like sheep they [the godless] are appointed for Sheol;
>> death shall be their shepherd,
> and the upright shall rule over them in the morning.
>> Their form shall be consumed in Sheol,
>> with no place to dwell.
> But God will ransom my soul from the power of Sheol,
>> for he will receive me.

> (Ps. 49:14-15)

The godly *will* be ransomed from the power of the grave; they will receive God's righteousness and will be received into God's presence forever. Many other Psalms likewise proclaim that glorious truth. But here, in Psalm 88, this man's great anxiety is that this will not be so for him. He fears that he is abandoned by God like those 'you remember no more' (5); he feels submerged under God's anger, His wrath 'lies heavy' and overwhelms him (7). It is not death he fears; it is damnation.

Looming hell

For any believer, this is a far, far worse darkness than the fear of natural death. He feels like his physical life may be drawing to a close: 'My life draws near to Sheol' (3). But his soul, his

---

11. Hebrews 9:27
12. Psalm 1:5-6.

whole being, is deeply troubled because of this great dread. He cannot face death with a steady eye; he cannot face death with peace because of *this* dread darkness. He fears he is lost, that his sin is still upon him, that he *will* be damned. His hope is quenched in that darkness. It is too late for me! he thinks: are your saving wonders known in the darkness? (12).

This is very often the great fear of the Christian believer who is overcome by the darkness of severe depressive illness, the dreadful anxiety that tortures their soul day and night. It is the nature of mental illness that the phenomenology of the symptoms, especially in psychosis, will tend to reflect the beliefs that are closest to a person's heart and soul, and for believers of course these are the things of God. And so, very often, a Christian who is suffering this way will be overwhelmed with a sense that they have committed 'the unpardonable sin', that they are beyond hope of grace. They may be tormented by terrible thoughts about their sin, about the devil, about hell. Sometimes it can make Christians believe that their problem is purely spiritual in nature, when in fact they do need the help of experienced doctors, as well as the support of God's people. God in His grace and mercy has given His people access to psychiatry and psychology, as well as to prayer, and we should be thankful for both, and not eschew the gifts of His common grace.

But of course it is not just those who are ill who can suffer these great anxieties about eternity. Lack of assurance has been a problem for many, many Christians all down the years. The Westminster Confession of Faith, (the standard of doctrine in my church), acknowledges this, although it asserts very strongly, against the Roman Catholic dogma of the day, that those who truly believe in the LORD Jesus may certainly be assured of their salvation – we can have 'an infallible assurance of faith'.[13] Nevertheless it also recognizes that even true

---

13. *Westminster Confession of Faith*, Chapter XVIII, Of Assurance of Grace and Salvation, Section II.

believers may have their assurance shaken and diminished in various ways – perhaps understandably, because of some sin or some great temptation, but also sometimes inexplicably. 'God withdrawing the light of his countenance and suffering even such as fear him to walk in darkness and to have no light.'[14] And we know that happens; sincere believers can feel the darkness of that dreadful anxiety: 'Am I really forgiven? Can I be sure? Perhaps I'm not really a real Christian. Maybe that *is* why God is not answering my prayers.' I'd be surprised if many of us hadn't thought that at some time or other, in times of great darkness, and if other foolish Christians – or foolish and wicked teachers – peddle a theology that reinforces the belief that if God doesn't answer prayer the way you want, then the problem *is* with you, and with your faith, that can, and does, sometimes lead people to real despair.

A cry of abandonment

Verses 13-18 certainly express despair, a daily cry of despairing abandonment which expresses the despairing darkness of a God who is hidden. The Psalmist is living a life of lonely desertion: 'O LORD, why do you go on casting my soul away? Why do you keep hiding your face from me?' (14).[15]

There is real desolation of despair in that cry. He is crying out for explanation – 'Why? Why won't you answer? Why won't you even explain why you are angry with me? Why have you abandoned me?' There are few things in life as desolating as having every attempt at communication you make with someone you love met with absolute silence: every call you make hung up on, every text, every email you send unanswered, every time you look at the person their eyes turn away. How much

---

14. *Westminster Confession of Faith*, Chapter XVIII, Of Assurance of Grace and Salvation, Section IV.

15. The language expresses the force of the present continuous tense in English.

more when it seems to be so with the God of our salvation: that *He* is silent and distant and absent.

There is a dark paradox here, is there not? God *is* absent, it seems. He hides Himself, He casts the Psalmist away from Him (14). And yet, He is *not* absent, because it is *He* (God Himself) who is afflicting him: 'I suffer *your* terrors...*your* wrath...*your* dreadful assaults' (15-16). God is absent for any *answers*, but He is very present for dreadful *affliction*. He is absent to give any *comfort*, but He is present to send *calamity*: 'your dreadful assaults destroy me' (16). The only response to his despairing prayer, as Derek Kidner says, is 'a rain of blows as unremitting as his cries':[16] 'They surround me like a flood all day long; they close in on me together' (17). God has abandoned him, it seems, and so has the whole world, even his nearest and dearest; he is shunned by his closest friends. His only companion now is the darkness (18).[17]

Unrelieved darkness

And that is the Psalm's last word. There is no turning point, no wonderful testimony here to prayers heard and answered, no return to songs of joy, only darkness – deep, dreadful, despairing darkness. This believer, a man committed to God and committed to persevering prayer:

> finds no remedial answers to suffering. The wrath of God (7), the alienation of friends, and inescapable (8) debilitating grief (9) fills the whole of life; the upward look sees only wrath; the inward look, terror; the outward look, present threats and absent friends (17-18) and the forward look, unrelieved darkness.[18]

---

16.   Kidner, *Psalms 73-150*, 318.

17.   'darkness has become my only companion' may be a better translation, as per the ESV footnote.

18.   Motyer, *The New Bible Commentary*, 542.

Perhaps you have felt like that at some time in your own life, possibly even recently. Maybe you have watched a loved one die slowly and painfully from some dreadful wasting disease, feeling utterly helpless as you have done so. Or you have come to terms with a sudden tragedy, the untimely death of a spouse or of a child. Or you have experienced your whole life apparently coming apart through the loss of your job or the collapse of your business, or your family battered and torn apart through the influence of drugs or alcohol, or through the bitter darkness of a marriage break up. Perhaps for you the agony has been an aching longing for the marriage partner who never came or the children never conceived. Or it may be any number of a thousand other sorrows, where every cry and prayer to God seemed met with this Divine silence.

Why? Why? 'Day and night...every day' your cry goes up constantly to God, and the only answer is... darkness: 'When I hoped for good, evil came, and when I waited for light, darkness came.'[19] That, too, was this Psalmist's deeply painful prayer.

A Deeply Pastoral Purpose

Why is it here, though, in our Bibles – such a sad and dark utterance? The answer is that it is written for us, for you and for me – 'written for our... encouragement', to help us in *our* times of darkness.[20] Indeed its very presence in the Psalter is evidence that God is *not* absent in our darkness but that He is present. He is present with words of mercy and grace to minister to us even in the deepest, darkest pit.

This Psalm has a deeply pastoral purpose. Like all the Scriptures, it brings us real help in trouble, real succour in our pain, real assurance even in our deepest darkness – because

---

19. Job 30:26.

20. Romans 15:4 reminds us that all the Old Testament finds its principal purpose in the Christian Church today, because it was 'written for our instruction that...through the encouragement of the Scriptures we might have hope.'

it speaks with real honesty about our experience, about this world, and about God Himself. There is no assurance, none at all, in self-deception, in the pretense of cloaking pain with happy songs. But there is great assurance in reality, and this Psalm bears clear testimony to real things in which we may find real reassurance.

Real sorrows

First, it tells us that there *are* real sorrows for a believer living in this cursed world. Suffering, even utterly dark and dreadful despair, is real, even for the most godly, wise, and mature believers.

When these things come upon Christians, it does not mean that they have just handled things badly, or made mistakes, or been foolish. Heman was full of wisdom; none other than Solomon was wiser, and yet he experienced this great darkness. And when such sorrows are real and dark, denial of that reality is utterly destructive. Trying to sing happy songs and convince yourself that all is well is no answer. (Secular science acknowledges this also; studies have shown that when feeling bad, listening to sad songs are better for your emotions than happy songs.[21])

Christians do face real sorrows, and they suffer from stresses and anxieties and depression and real darkness. Very often *our* darkness is worse because of the sense of spiritual failure that is added to it, the feeling that as Christians we should somehow not face these things. That only adds to the despair, and so we *need* the dark reality of this Psalm, we need the witness of Heman's deeply painful prayer. It tells us that, yes, believers, even wise, godly, mature believers can face deep and dreadful and despairing darkness.[22] The Bible is real about sorrow and

21. See, for example, Kawakami A, Furukawa K, Katahira K and Okanoya K, 'Sad music induces pleasant emotion', *Frontiers in Psychology*, Volume 4 (June 2013): 311.

22. Similarly, we need the book of Ecclesiastes to remind us that we live, even as believers, with mortality that we cannot control, and with mysteries

sufferings in our lives and what a blessed relief and a comfort that is to us. Health will and does fail. Death will come to greatest and least alike. Friends will sometimes abandon us. Other calamities will happen. 'In the world,' said the LORD Jesus Christ, 'you will have tribulation.'[23] Spirit-filled believers will be marked by groaning until the very end, says Paul in his great chapter on the Spirit-filled life (Rom. 8). That does not mean that you are lost; it does not mean that God has abandoned you, even if it seems to be so. Nor does it mean that a loved one of yours is lost or abandoned by God – even if they are engulfed in deep darkness and believe so strongly that they are lost that in their confusion and darkness, they try to end it all to escape their pain, and even succeed.

Real songs

There are real sorrows, and there will be real darkness, in the Christian life. That is why God has given us this prayer, and others like it, as real songs for believers in times of darkness.

This Psalm is for using; it is why it is here. In Psalms like this, God Himself has given us 'the vocabulary, grammar and syntax necessary to lay open your heart before God in lamentation.'[24] This song is here to help us to know how to cope and what to say in our own times of suffering and grief and heartbreak, and to help others know how to deal with *their* times of darkness too. It teaches us that it is alright to cry to God, to be honest with Him. It's alright to lament, to weep, to express darkness and despair. It's not wrong *not* to want to be a jolly Christian when you are sad. It's not wrong; it is right? That kind of pretence is so destructive of real faith.

---

that we cannot comprehend in this cursed world under the sun, and the way of wisdom – and joy – lies not in trying to deny this, but accepting the limitations of our humanity and living with expectations for everything which is temporal, not ultimate.

23. John 16:33.

24. Trueman, "Miserable Christians", 3.

But real prayer like this – expressing deep pain and sorrow openly in words like this – is what *guards* real faith, and does bring reassurance even in the deepest darkness. 'LORD, why *don't* you hear me? Listen to me, *please*, LORD. Why are you *doing* this, why are *you* assaulting me?' Even to pray like that is an acknowledgement that you know it is *not* just mindless chance and misfortune that is happening to you. It is to say that God *is* real, that God *is* sovereign, that things are *not* outwith His control, that even if we cannot fathom it, He is still the one who *we need* to do something about it. So, we cry out *to the LORD!*

Even in our darkest times, deep down in our hearts, we know God is sovereign. *That's* our problem! That's *why* we are in agony; that is why we get angry with God. That's why we accuse God: 'Why *don't* you listen? Why *don't* you change things?' But there is an assurance, paradoxically, even in our sense of abandonment, even in our sense of God's absence. We would not keep on praying like that, remonstrating with God, unless God had planted real persevering faith in our hearts, by His Spirit. So in the very agony of our sense of forsakenness, is a very real assurance of the certainty of our un-forsakenness: we are still naming Him as LORD, the LORD, the Covenant God, 'God of my salvation'.

The Real Saviour

And so, when we are in the midst of real sorrows, if we will let the Psalmist's words and prayers lead us in this real song that reaches out in trust, even in the deepest darkness, we will find that He is leading us inexorably to the real Saviour – to a God whose name really is salvation. 'O LORD, God of my salvation' he cries in verse 1 – 'O LORD, God *my Yeshua'* as the Hebrew says. That surely brings it home to us so wonderfully, and so clearly, for we would pronounce that name, 'my Yeshua,' as 'my Jesus.'

God has given us the very words to pray in our darkness because He Himself knows these words. Not only did His Spirit inspire the Psalmist, but in a deeper sense these are *His* words, the words of the God who became our Saviour, ultimately in the person of His Son, the LORD Jesus. 'In the days of his flesh', says Hebrews 5:7, Jesus 'offered up prayers and supplications with loud cries and tears to Him who was able to save Him from death, and He was heard because of His reverence'. But in the Garden of Gethsemane, He was answered only with deep, despairing darkness when *He* cried in *deep agony*, 'Let this cup pass from me';[25] and when He cried again in *dread* and *anxiety*, 'If this cannot pass unless I drink it, "your will be done,"' as He contemplated the cup of the fury and the wrath of God upon *Him*.[26] *A*nd, above all on the cross, when He cried out in the words of Psalm 22, which echo so closely the words here in Psalm 88:14, 'Why have you forsaken me'?[27] – surely that was a cry of *despairing abandonment*, as the insults showered over Him, as the terrors of hell engulfed Him, as the wrath of God swept over Him to destroy Him, and the deep, dreadful darkness of despair closed in on Him altogether.

His prayer, from inside the darkness, for us

Yes, our God knows this prayer. He knows these agonised cries *from the inside*. In the LORD who is our salvation, our Yeshua, 'we do not have a high priest who is unable to sympathize with our weaknesses' – or our darknesses – 'but who, in every respect, has been tempted as we are'[28] – and, indeed, with an infinity of suffering, far deeper and more terrible. And so, whatever your darknesses or mine (and they *may* be very real, and deep, and terrible), as you cry out to God in agony, and in

---

25. Matthew 26:39.
26. Matthew 26:42.
27. Matthew 27:46
28. Hebrews 4:15.

anxiety, and perhaps with a sense of being abandoned, when you wait for light and only darkness seems to come, let that darkness lead you to the darkness of Calvary. Let it lead you to Jesus, the God of our salvation, who won your salvation through His own abandonment there on the cross for you. Let the darkness itself proclaim to your troubled soul the *light* of the assurance that His glorious gospel brings: that through *His* infinite suffering in darkness, *you* have a promise of infinite light. 'Whoever follows me,' says the Lord Jesus 'will not walk in darkness' forever, but 'will have the light of life'.[29]

Your darkness cannot be infinite, precisely because His *was*. Jesus, the name of our Salvation, endured that darkness for you, and indeed for all who love Him. And so,

> When we in darkness walk,
> nor feel the heavenly flame;
> *then* is the time to trust our God
> and rest upon *his name*.[30]

---

29. John 8:12.

30. Augustus Toplady, *Your harps, ye trembling saints* (1772).

Safe in the Shadow of the Almighty

Psalm 91 – a song of Promise

¹ He who dwells in the shelter of the Most High
    will abide in the shadow of the Almighty.
² I will say to the LORD, "My refuge and my fortress,
    my God, in whom I trust."

³ For he will deliver you from the snare of the fowler
    and from the deadly pestilence.
⁴ He will cover you with his pinions,
    and under his wings you will find refuge;
    his faithfulness is a shield and buckler.
⁵ You will not fear the terror of the night,
    nor the arrow that flies by day,
⁶ nor the pestilence that stalks in darkness,
    nor the destruction that wastes at noonday.

⁷ A thousand may fall at your side,
    ten thousand at your right hand,
    but it will not come near you.
⁸ You will only look with your eyes
    and see the recompense of the wicked.

⁹ Because you have made the LORD your dwelling place—

the Most High, who is my refuge—
[10] no evil shall be allowed to befall you,
     no plague come near your tent.

[11] For he will command his angels concerning you
     to guard you in all your ways.
[12] On their hands they will bear you up,
     lest you strike your foot against a stone.
[13] You will tread on the lion and the adder;
     the young lion and the serpent you
     will trample underfoot.

[14] "Because he holds fast to me in love, I will deliver him;
     I will protect him, because he knows my name.
[15] When he calls to me, I will answer him;
     I will be with him in trouble;
     I will rescue him and honor him.
[16] With long life I will satisfy him
     and show him my salvation."

Psalm 91

We cannot be sure who wrote this Psalm, but it is likely it comes from Moses, at least originally. [1] Psalm 90 is entitled 'a prayer of Moses, the man of God', and with it Psalm 91 forms an introduction to the fourth 'book' of the Psalter whose focus is on 'the ancient reality that God Himself is His people's dwelling place and that Yahweh is their king.'[2] Book 3 of the Psalter (Ps. 73-89) testifies to the apparent defeat of God's messianic kingdom, His people and their king dragged into exile. It culminates in the forlorn cry: 'How long, O LORD?

---

1.   The Jewish Talmud attributes Psalms 90-101 to Moses. Since no other author is mentioned until Psalm 101, it is possible these all continue the prayers of Moses.

2.   O. Palmer Robertson, *The Flow of the Psalms*, 147. The word 'dwelling place' ('habitation') is used regularly as the place where the LORD Himself dwells, and both Psalm 90 & 91 emphasise that the LORD Himself is the eternal 'dwelling place' of safety and security for His people – 90:1; c.f. 91:1, 9.

Will you hide yourself forever?... Where is your steadfast love of old?'[3] But now, Book 4 'beginning dramatically with Psalm 90, celebrates the LORD himself as the eternal dwelling place of his people (Ps. 90:1). Even back to the time of Moses the man of God... God has continued to be his people's secure dwelling place.'[4]

Psalm 91 is a Psalm of promise, all about being safe in the shadow of the Almighty God. It is full of promises from beginning to end, about what God does, and what God *will* do for His people. These promises are proclaimed by the Psalmist, backed by his own personal testimony: 'This is *my* God I'm speaking about,' he is saying (2, 9). They are also promises affirmed by God Himself – six times the LORD Himself speaks, affirming 'I will' keep these extraordinary promises to His believing child (14-16).

Promising too much?

There is a problem, however, as we approach a Psalm like this: is the Psalm promising too much? It does seem to be proclaiming a life that is utterly charmed, free from all illness and from all misfortune. It seems to offer a life without sickness, injury, and poverty, only health, prosperity, and wealth – and a guaranteed long future retirement. Certainly there are those who would claim that this is exactly what is promised and that if this is not your personal experience, the problem is yours; you just do not have enough faith. That may be because you haven't given enough money to the church to prove your faith. So, what you really need to do is open your wallet – then surely the prosperity as described in this Psalm will begin to flow, in direct proportion to your giving. Needless to say, pastors of churches that proclaim this message do tend to be very prosperous, even if the congregation members are not.

---

3. Psalm 89:46, 49.
4. Robertson, *The Flow of the Psalms*, 150.

This so-called 'prosperity gospel' is rife in the world today, especially in parts of Africa, but it is very common in the West too. Sometimes it is crass, and sometimes more sophisticated, but it is very common. Less common, but nevertheless present in some places, are more bizarre groups of people, who take a promise like 'the serpent you will trample underfoot' (13) in such a way as drives them to insist that snake-handling is an integral part of worship. They quite literally stand in pits full of rattlesnakes and handle them, claiming divine protection; some even demand snake handling as evidence of salvation. Many, of course, are bitten; some of them die. But that does not seem to deter them, much as it may astonish us.

What are we to say to a Psalm that may seem to give support to such views?

Demonic twisting of Scripture

What we can say quite categorically is that such an interpretation of this Psalm is not merely mistaken, it is positively demonic. That is not my opinion, but the clear verdict of Scripture itself, which records the devil himself using this Psalm in exactly that way when quoting it to Jesus during His temptation in the wilderness (Matt. 4:6). The devil tempts Jesus to *presume* upon God's promises of protection, and so to jump off the pinnacle of the temple. 'For it is written…"his angels…will bear you up,"' he says, quoting Psalm 91:11-12 to imply that no physical harm will come to Jesus if he jumps off a high building. But Jesus rebukes the devil sharply. He says, 'Again it is written, "You shall *not* put the LORD your God to the test"', a quote from Deuteronomy 6:16, referring to Israel's presumptuous testing of the LORD in the wilderness when they demanded water and said, 'Is the LORD really among us? Let him show himself.'

So, according to Jesus Himself, that kind of misuse of this Psalm is devilish; it is sinful and presumptuous to test God, demanding that He serve us. But these promises are not to lead us to unbelieving *testing* of God, but rather to faithful *trusting* in God's unseen power and goodness and care – even in the midst of physical hardship, like the testing in the wilderness, where Jesus Himself was *not* spared. Matthew tells us angels did indeed come and minister to Jesus, but not to remove the hardship; rather they came to strengthen Him in the midst of His obedient and trusting faith.[5] Thus He did tread the tempter down, to 'trample underfoot' the Serpent – the devil – who departed from Him. It is surely no accident that later, also, it was in Gethsemane – when Jesus was in agony, contemplating the cross ahead of Him and praying 'Father, if you are willing, remove this cup… nevertheless, not my will but yours, be done', and where He persevered through that intense trial and agony of grief – that again 'there appeared to him an angel from heaven, strengthening him.'[6] There, once more, we see the absolute antithesis of presumptuous demands for peace and prosperity; once more the Serpent He trampled underfoot.

It is not surprising that the devil stopped his quote to Jesus from Psalm 91 at verse 12. No doubt the words of verse 13, 'the serpent you will trample underfoot', were much too close to the bone for 'that ancient serpent, who is called the devil and Satan, the deceiver of the whole world' as Revelation 12:9 calls him. How he loves to deceive by misusing and misconstruing God's own words of promise! He truly is, as Jesus said, a murderous 'liar and the father of lies', and has been from the beginning (just read Genesis 3).[7] So we must not fall prey to the devil's deception and twisting of a Psalm like this. If we do, we are liable to lose faith in God, because we will presume from God all kinds of things that He has never in fact promised to us; when we do not receive them, we will begin to give up on God, thinking He has no power. That, sadly, is the story of many

---

5. Matthew 4:11.

6. Luke 22:42-43.

7. John 8:44.

who were lured by the prosperity gospel, which is one of Satan's biggest lies, and it has ruined many lives.

Promising too little?

But then if that is not the kind of prosperity of which this Psalm is speaking, what *is* it speaking about? Does it actually promise anything at all? Or is it, as some commentators think, that the Psalmist's faith 'grows a bit exuberant at this point'; that these extraordinary statements mean simply that God *can* deliver people from dire straits, that *sometimes* He does, but that often He does not. That all verses like verse 7, 'a thousand may fall at your side... but it will not come near you', state is that 'it is possible for God to defend His own in cases of seemingly inescapable dangers, and He will frequently do so.'[8] In other words, when it says, 'but it will not come near you,' it really means 'except on the occasions when it *does* come near you'. That is hardly very comforting, is it? Are we really to think that God's promises then are no more reliable than a politician's? Is He going to have to make apologetic videos saying, 'I'm sorry, I misled you', as Nick Clegg the one-time leader of the Liberal Democrats infamously once had to do for the British Public?

The problem that scholars who write like this are trying to address is a real one, because verse 10 seems utterly definite: '*no evil* shall be allowed to befall you'. And yet if we are honest as Christians, we look around and see troubles everywhere, often very close to the 'tents' of our own lives. So, if it does mean something real – if it is a solid promise from God that we can rely on, always, not just in a 'generally speaking, most of the time this happens' sort of way – what can this mean for us?

The key lies in a careful understanding of both the language and imagery of the Psalm, and also its true focus, which is clearly on the great matters of ultimate importance in life:

---

8. H.C. Leupold, *Exposition of The Psalms* (Welwyn: Evangelical Press, 1977), 653.

ultimate destruction and deliverance, the ultimate recompense of the wicked and the ultimate rescue of the godly. That is what the Psalmist is really concerned with here, and we need to understand this, and not misapply it in a merely trivial way. This is a Psalm that *does* promise something surely and certainly to the believer. It promises that they will not ultimately be overcome by evil but they *will be* overcomers; they will be those who know now, and forever, true life – the life that is truly knowing God forever, the life that *is* seeing His salvation. We could read the last verse this way,

> With *true* (or abundant) life I will satisfy him,
> showing him my salvation.

Promising the life of salvation

This *is* a Psalm of promise. It promises that for all those who 'dwell in the shelter of the Most High', for all who 'abide in the shadow of the Almighty', there is absolute safety – ultimately and forever. All such have a promise from God's own mouth of a real and *permanent salvation* (14-16). Therefore, the Psalmist can confidently promise to others what he knows to be true for himself: that to make this God your dwelling place is to know both His *personal shelter* in the face of all punishment for wickedness (1-8), and His *present strengthening* in the face of all the powers of evil (9-13).

So, let us look carefully at what this Psalm is really teaching about: the life of salvation, which is the life lived safe in the shadow of the Almighty. We shall begin at the end, with verses 14-16, because there we have God's own voice, and indeed verse 16 is a key verse which, if we can understand it properly, will open up the whole Psalm to us.

A Permanent Salvation

These verses give God's own promise that he who abides with Him will know real and permanent salvation. His promise is for *permanent life*, a life that will be permanent, ultimately *with* God forever.

The Psalm describes a life permanently *secure* under God's *preservation* – 'I will deliver him; I will protect him' (14); 'I will be with him… I will rescue him and honour him' (15). Moreover, it is a life that is permanently *satisfied* in God's *presence* – 'With [lit] *length of days* I will satisfy him and show him my salvation' (16, emphasis added). Though perhaps addressed directly here to Israel's king, as representative of the people of God, this is the same promise of God's permanent, preserving presence given to Abraham back at the very beginning: that the LORD would be ever-present to bless him and his offspring, blessing those who blessed them and cursing those who cursed them (Gen. 12:2-4). It is the sure promise of God 'guaranteed to *all* his offspring', and we have the wonderful confirmation that all who are in Christ by faith 'are Abraham's offspring, heirs according to promise.'[9] Verse 16 sums that up succinctly here as the life of permanent *satisfaction* and of *salvation*.

Verse 16 is key, and we really do need to understand it. If it is simply 'long life' that is being promised here, as most English translations suggest, we must ask, '*do* the godly always live a long earthly life?' Clearly that is not so; many great saints have died very young. Is this, then, just a generalization: if you live a godly, circumspect life then you will *tend* to live longer than the dissolute? No doubt there is some truth in that, but it is hardly a way around what appears as a very definite promise. More literally, the phrase says, 'With *length of days* I will satisfy him'. In some places that can reasonably be translated as 'long life', but very often – particularly in the Psalms and other poetry – it clearly means something very different from that. The nearby Psalm 93:5 gives a handy example: 'Holiness befits your house, O LORD, *forevermore*,' [emphasis added] ('*for endless days*', NIV; '*for ever*', KJV). This literally translates to '*for length of days*', and is the same phrase used here in

<hr>

9.   Romans 4:16; Galatians 3:29.

Psalm 91:16. Similarly, and very familiar, is the last verse of Psalm 23, 'I shall dwell in the house of the LORD *forever*', where the ESV footnote notes the Hebrew reads literally '*for length of days*', again the same as here in Psalm 91:16. Another place we find this phrase – where it cannot possibly mean long *earthly* life – is in Isaiah 53:10, in the famous Servant Song. We are told that after the Servant of the LORD dies, after He gives His life as an offering for sin, 'he shall see his offspring; he shall *prolong his days*' – literally he shall have '*length of days*'. The Messiah will have life. He will 'prosper' and 'be satisfied' in *endless* days, *beyond* His physical death.

The path of true life

This same understanding of true 'life' is prominent in the Wisdom books like Proverbs and Ecclesiastes, where 'life' very rarely just means mere clinical life. It means much more; it conveys the abundance of *life lived in fellowship with the LORD*, a living relationship that will *not* end with clinical death, but stretches out beyond, forever. This is a life that is in stark contrast to the 'cutting off' of the wicked in death: 'It will not be well with the wicked, neither will he prolong his days [have *length of days*]… because he does not fear before God'.[10] But by contrast, 'In the path of righteousness is *life*, and in that pathway there is *no death*'.[11] For Proverbs, it is the *wise* who know the LORD, for whom 'there will be a future', whose 'hope will not be cut off'. By contrast, 'the evil man has *no* future; the lamp of the wicked will be put out'.[12]

So we can see that what God *is* promising here in Psalm 91:16 is real salvation, which is real and permanent *life in fellowship with this God*, the God who gives permanent security

10. Ecclesiastes 8:13.

11. Proverbs 12:28.

12. Proverbs 24:14, 20. The real death spoken of here is the antithesis of the unending real life which is experienced by those who know and fear the LORD; to be cut off forever from the source of life, God Himself, is to experience forever the punishment of death, c.f. Matthew 25:46.

and permanent and ultimate satisfaction. Perhaps one last reference from another Psalm is clearest of all, where David is rejoicing in the salvation that God has granted him, personally. He articulates his own experience, saying:

'He asked *life* of you; you gave it to him,
length of days forever and ever.
His glory is great through your *salvation*'
(Ps. 21:4-5, emphasis added)

Life, length of days, salvation – the parallelism of the poetry makes it absolutely clear that for David these are all one and the same thing. 'I will show him my *salvation*' says the LORD here in verse 16 – which is true *life*, abundant life, life in all its fullness, life forever and ever in the presence of God. It *is* an absolute promise of permanent salvation – life that will never be snuffed out by mere physical death. Those who make the LORD their 'dwelling place' (9) or, in the language of Proverbs 'continue in the fear of the LORD' have a sure promise: 'surely there is a future and your hope will not be cut off'.[13] That is what Psalm 91 is promising.

This is what the whole world is seeking, and has been since the beginning of time: abundant life. We want life that is more than just mundane and miserable, life that has meaning, life that has hope and, above all, life that is not stolen by the great thief: death. An artist once said, with somewhat dark humour, 'I do not want to achieve immortality through my work; I want to achieve it by *not dying*' [emphasis added]. Well here is a promise of exactly that, to all who will listen and heed its call. It is no secret, though it is found in 'the secret place of the Most High'.[14] For this secret place – this 'shelter' – has been proclaimed aloud publicly by the LORD Himself, and by the Psalmist, here, as an invitation: if you will make *my* God *your*

---

13.   Prov. 23:17-18.

14.   as the KJV translates verse 1, rather literalistically, but nevertheless beautifully.

God, all this can be *yours* – 'he will deliver *you*' (3). This is the message of the whole Psalm.

A Personal Shelter

The message is so clear in verses 1-8 where the Psalmist bears his own personal testimony to God's promise to be a real personal shelter. His promise is of a *protected life*, protected ultimately *by* God.

The Lord 'is *my* refuge and *my* fortress' [emphasis added], says the Psalmist, because of the kind of God He is. These great names of God in verses 1-2 describe His nature. He is the Most High God (*El Elyon*), towering above all others and cutting every threat right down to size.[15] He is God Almighty (*El Shaddai*), the all-sufficient God who kept Jacob through all his wanderings.[16] He is the Lord (*YHWH*), the covenant God, the great I AM,[17] who will be everything that His people always need Him to be, ever true to every promise He gives. And, says the Psalmist, He is *my* God, a personal God; He intimately knows me as His very own. It is being in *His* shelter, in *His* hidden care and under *His* shadow that you will find permanent protection from all harm.

Verse 4 is a wonderful verse: it speaks both of the beautiful tenderness, and the battle-ready toughness, of God's protection. I have visited many castles and fortresses, and they are certainly very strong and safe; but they are often rough, harsh places. God's shelter is no less tough. His faithfulness is 'a shield and buckler' – solid body armour. But do you see the imagery? The Psalmist claims that 'He will cover you with his pinions,

---

15. Genesis 14:22.

16. Genesis 28:3.

17. Exodus 3:15. When God reveals Himself to Moses at the burning bush in naming Himself YHWH (Lord), there is a close connection and play the Hebrew verb 'to be' (HAYAH) in the previous verse, where God says to Moses, 'I am who I am', or 'I will be who I will be'. The sense seems to be that all the assurance and hope and certainty of the promise of God's presence with His people always is summed up in this one word – the covenant name YHWH.

and under his wings you will find refuge'. Inside *His* shelter it is as soft and comfortable as an eiderdown! The LORD is pictured here as a mother bird tenderly protecting her chicks from every possible harm, near to her body in the warmth and comfort of her own heart. There is nothing hard and rough about God's protection of His people. In his great song in Deuteronomy 32:11, Moses likens God's care of His people to that of an eagle: powerful and strong to protect against all foes, yet bearing its young tenderly on its own feathers.

The plots of the wicked

But protection from what? Verse 3 speaks of God's rescue from the plots of the wicked. The imagery here is very common in the Psalms: the 'snare/trap of the fowler', and the 'deadly pestilence'.[18] A better translation of the latter expression here may be (as with the Greek Old Testament) 'the deadly *word*'; that is, the traps, the words of temptation, the powerful lures which, as Derek Kidner says, threaten to 'entangle our affairs' or 'compromise our loyalty' to God.[19] The whole Bible warns of many snares and traps that can lead us to ruin. Moses warned constantly of the snares of pagan religion that would lead His people away to destruction. The Proverbs are always warning of snares: the snare of the adulteress, the snare of the fool's lips, the snare of the lure of wealth. The apostle Paul similarly speaks of snares: snares of riches, the many snares and traps of the devil's which can lead to ruin. And only the LORD's shelter can protect from such snares, from such plots of the wicked.

The punishment of the wicked

But the main emphasis in these verses lies in verses 5-8, where the Psalmist promises something very important indeed:

---

18.   We find very similar language in Psalm 124 and Psalm 140.

19.   Derek Kidner, *Psalms 73-150*, 332. The Hebrew word translated 'pestilence' has the same consonants as that meaning 'word', and so is identical in the original text.

a refuge from the punishment of the wicked. You will not fear 'the terror of the night', nor 'the arrow', 'the pestilence', 'the destruction.' Thousands will fall all around you but to *you* [it is emphatic] it will not come near (7). What is all this horror talking about? Verse 8 sums it up; it is the 'recompense' – the just punishment – 'of the wicked' he is referring to. You will see it, but you will never suffer it; if God is your personal shelter, you will not experience His punishment of the wicked.

The language of these verses is evocative of the plagues God sent upon Egypt in the book of Exodus., as well as some of the judgments God sent on His own unbelieving people in the desert, for their sin and their rebellion. Think of the plague of the fiery serpents in Numbers 21, or the great destruction in Numbers 25 when thousands were judged for their idolatry to the Baals of Peor.[20] Verse 10 speaks about tents, and the imagery does perhaps picture a people on a journey facing many disasters, many foes. The language is of a supernatural plague of destruction which is totally under God's control and which brings a just judgment – recompense – on the wicked, but keeps His own trusting people in total safety, just like the Passover, when every single home in the whole land of Egypt suffered the avenging angel of God except those that were *sheltered* under the blood daubed on the lintels and the doorposts, the blood of the Passover lamb. And in just this same way it shall be when God judges the whole world forever. 'Those who dwell under the *shelter* of my God,' says the Psalmist 'shall not fear that day.'

This is a very common theme in the Psalms, and a potent source of comfort for God's people. God *will* judge the wicked ultimately, even when it seems He is not judging them now. Psalm 37 is a classic example:

20.　There is much in the language which echoes the language used in Exodus to Deuteronomy, which would be unsurprising if Moses is the author of this Psalm.

Turn away from evil and do good;
    so shall you dwell forever.
For the Lord loves justice,
    he will not forsake his saints.
They are preserved forever,
    but the children of *the wicked shall be cut off…*

Wait for the Lord and keep his way,
    and he will exalt you to inherit the land;
    you will look on *when the wicked are cut off.*'

                  (Ps. 37:27-28, 34, emphasis added)

The coming of God's judgment is a great comfort to the oppressed when they see the wicked triumphing now; He *will* bring recompense to the wicked – in perfect, just and wise judgment.

But this reality can also be a great source of fear, even for believers, because we know our own guilt, and the sin in our own hearts. In fact it may only be *because* we know God's truth that we do fear; the world arrogantly ignores God, saying, 'There will be no judgment, we *do not* fear.' But we Christians *do* fear because we see our own guilt, and we feel it, maybe in the darkness of night, with its terrors; or perhaps in the weakness of illness or in old age; or most of all, in the aftermath of some lapse into sin. And we may wonder 'can God really turn aside His judgment? Maybe I *will* be punished with the recompense my sin deserves!'

Or perhaps, having never really given Christian faith a thought, you are reading this book because something has happened in your life – maybe you have been diagnosed with some illness – and you have started to fear death, and what might come afterwards. Like Hamlet, you fear:

'the dread of something after death,
the undiscovered country from whose bourn
no traveller returns…'

Thus, as Shakespeare says, 'conscience does make cowards of us all'. [21]

But the Psalmist offers a promise to all who fear these things: if you trust in my God, in whom I trust, He *will be* your personal shelter. He will be your shelter from all the just punishment for wickedness and sin. You will *not* fear the plague of His wrath; 'to you it will *not* come near.' Fear not.

'Fear Not!' is the great clarion call in the Bible which God loves to sound to people whose faith is faltering: *'Fear not! For I have redeemed you, I have called you by name, you are mine,'* says the LORD, *'...the flame shall not consume you.'*[22] *'Fear not,* little flock, for it is your Father's good pleasure to give you the kingdom,'* says the LORD Jesus Christ.[23] The Psalmist notes that if you are a believer you 'will not fear the terror' (5), and 'will only look with your eyes and see the recompense of the wicked' (8), not because of your superior righteousness, but because you have a refuge: the real *personal shelter* who is Himself the assurance of a real and *permanent salvation*.

A Present Strengthening

And because this is true, 'because you have made the LORD your dwelling place – the Most High, who is my refuge', says the Psalmist (9), you can also rejoice in the promise of a real present strengthening. God's promise is for a *prevailing life*, the life that prevails ultimately *with* God.

Verses 10 -13 tell us that through God's powerful providence you will be kept amid all the *perils* of evil, amid the stones that strew your way throughout life in this fallen world (12); and you will be conquerors over all the *powers* of evil, even the Serpent who strikes at your heel (13). Again verse 10 is absolute – *'No evil* shall be allowed to befall you.' Notice he does not say no affliction, no hardship, no struggles in life, but no *evil*. He

---

21. William Shakespeare, *Hamlet*, Act 3 Scene 1.

22. Isaiah 43:1-2 (emphasis added).

23. Luke 12:32.

is not saying that your life will be charmed and exempt from all perils; in fact, he says plainly there *will* be stones along the path, and the serpent *will* stalk your path. But what he is saying is that no such perils, or powers, will be allowed to ultimately floor those who have this God as their refuge.

Rather, He is a God who uses even the worst powers of evil, the worst evil of men and of devils, and turns it to the good of those who are 'called according to his purpose'.[24] 'You meant *evil* against me, but God meant it for *good*', indeed for a great purpose of salvation, is how Joseph put it to the brothers who had done him such wickedness.[25] The whole host of heaven's angels are at work, says the Psalmist, making sure this is so; they are there to keep you, to guard you in all your ways (11). Moses knew all about angels. God gave him a promise in these very words in Exodus 23:20-22, that there would be an angel going ahead to keep them, to guard them, all the way to the Promised Land. And in the New Testament, Hebrews 1:14 tells us that the angels are 'ministering spirits' sent by God to help those that He is saving, to 'bear them up', just as verse 12 says here – precisely because there will be many stones in the path, many perils of evil to encounter in a fallen world.

That is the reality of the life of faith. It is a hard struggle with a multitude of things that *could* floor us. But we shall *not* stumble so as to fall completely! That is the constant teaching of the Biblical gospel.

When someone is the LORD's, 'though he fall, he shall *not* be cast headlong, for the LORD upholds his hand' says Psalm 37:24. Whereas 'the wicked *stumble* in times of calamity', Proverbs 24:16 declares that 'the righteous falls seven times and *rises* again' (emphasis added). 'We are afflicted in every way, but not crushed, perplexed, but not driven to despair, persecuted, but not forsaken; struck down, but not destroyed' says Paul to

24. Romans 8:28.
25. Genesis 50:20.

the Corinthian church.[26] Why? Because what this Psalm tells us is true! 'No evil shall be *allowed* to befall you' (10), because 'for those who love God all things work together for *good*, for those who are called according to his purpose'.[27] And that *good*, Paul tells us there, is our being conformed into the image of the LORD Jesus Christ: that in Him we may prevail, as He prevailed over every *peril* of evil, and that through Him we also might conquer every *power* of evil, treading down the Lion and the Serpent, and trampling them underfoot.

Trampling the Serpent underfoot

You only have to read other Psalms (like Psalm 58) and many other Scriptures, to know that what is meant here in verse 13 of this Psalm is nothing to do with bizarre snake handling, and everything to do with bold Serpent crushing! The devil is the roaring Lion seeking to devour, the cunning Serpent seeking to deceive.[28] But you will not just survive them, says the Psalmist, you will conquer them: all the powers of evil 'you will trample underfoot.' The Psalmists and the prophets longed for the coming day when at last, as God promised, the Serpent would be destroyed forever, on the great day of the LORD. 'In that day', Isaiah cried,

> the LORD with his hard and great and strong sword will punish Leviathan the fleeing serpent, Leviathan the twisting serpent, and he will slay the dragon that is in the sea.[29]

And so it was, at last, that the Son of God appeared 'to destroy the works of the devil'.[30] God's promised Messiah King, in whose triumphant faithfulness verses 14-16 of this Psalm find their

---

26. 2 Corinthians 4:8-9.
27. Romans. 8:28 (emphasis added).
28. 1 Peter 5:8; 2 Corinthians 11:3; Revelation 12:9; Genesis 3:13.
29. Isaiah 27:1.
30. 1 John 3:8.

truest fulfilment, has crushed the Serpent, bringing salvation to all His own. As Isaiah promised, having 'out of the anguish of his soul' made 'an offering for sin', He has risen victorious to 'prolong his days' in endless life, to 'see and be satisfied' in the salvation of all 'his offspring' who share in the spoil of his victory.[31] Thus Christ's apostle can promise Christian believers, with absolute assurance, that 'the God of peace shall soon crush Satan under *your* feet'.[32]

God's promise to those who are His is for a life that shall prevail over all evil, and so we can be assured of a *present strengthening*. 'No evil shall be allowed to befall you': nothing in the path of your life will ever make you stumble so as to fall permanently if you abide under His shadow. Though your path in life be full of stones and rocks in this fallen world, that is God's promise! No evil power, not even the devil himself, shall overcome you!

So do not despair. Even if it seems like you *are* surrounded by roaring lions and fiery serpents right now in your Christian life, it does not mean that God has abandoned you; it does not mean that you are coming under His judgment at last. How could it, when Jesus Himself was faced with all of these things and much, much more? No, in all these very things – in every affliction – He will not allow evil to befall us, but will turn everything to His ultimate glory in Christ; in all these things we are conquerors, and 'more than conquerors, through him who loved us'.[33] 'You can trust this God, *my* God' says the Psalmist. And you can be assured of His present strengthening in your life today, to keep you in all your ways in this evil world, and to make you conquer every evil power that is against your soul – 'the young Lion and the Serpent you will trample underfoot.'

---

31. Isaiah 53:10-12.

32. Romans 16:20 (emphasis added).

33. Romans 8:37.

The promise of life in all its fullness

This *is* a Psalm of promise. It holds out the certain promise of a life that is *protected* from all punishment against sin, of a life that *prevails* over every power of evil, and a life that is *permanent* in the presence of God Himself. If you are a Christian believer, aren't you glad that you have this God as your shelter, your hiding place, your dwelling place?

But perhaps you are *not* sure that you *are* a real Christian. And you are wondering 'How do I *find* that refuge: that shelter, that strengthening, that salvation?' The good news is it is not complicated! Verse 14 could not be clearer. This blessing is for *all* who *hold fast* to the LORD in love. It is for all who know *His name*; it is for all who will *call to Him*. These He will always answer – to satisfy with everlasting *'length of days'* seeing His great salvation. The LORD Jesus Christ came into our world to make known that name to all, and to continue to make it known. He came to bring *life*, in all its fullness, which is to know the Father through Him.[34] 'This is the will of my father', says the LORD Jesus, 'that everyone who looks on the Son and believes in him should have eternal life, and I will raise him up on the last day'.[35]

> 'With endless days I will satisfy him,
> and show him my salvation.'

That is a sure and certain promise from the lips of the Most High God.

---

34. John 17:3.
35. John 6:40.

Where Does Your Help Come From?

Psalm 121 – a song of pilgrimage

A Song of Ascents.

[1] I lift up my eyes to the hills.
    From where does my help come?
[2] My help comes from the LORD,
    who made heaven and earth.

[3] He will not let your foot be moved;
    he who keeps you will not slumber.
[4] Behold, he who keeps Israel
    will neither slumber nor sleep.

[5] The LORD is your keeper;
    the LORD is your shade on your right hand.
[6] The sun shall not strike you by day,
    nor the moon by night.

[7] The LORD will keep you from all evil;
    he will keep your life.
[8] The LORD will keep your going out and your coming in
    from this time forth and forevermore.

Psalm 121

In our family, this has been a Psalm often read at a time of parting or journeying. It is natural at such times to feel certain anxieties and fears, to sense a need for help, and to want to pray – especially if that parting is a significant one from loved ones. Maybe it is a young child going off to a summer camp for the very first time; perhaps it is an older teenager leaving home to begin university or go on a gap year; or it could be a loved one who is emigrating to a country far away across the ocean. Often these kinds of partings and journeyings bring into sharp focus the world's bigness, and our smallness by comparison – the size and scope of the threats of this world, over against our own sense of vulnerability and weakness. It brings home to us our lack of power to overcome, to give protection, to control things. Once we begin to think like that, we realize just how helpless we are.

This Psalm is a song of pilgrimage, of journeying. You see from the title it is the second of a group of fifteen Psalms called Songs of Ascents.[1] Literally the word 'ascents' means steps or stairs, and although we cannot be entirely sure, it does seem likely that this is a collection of Psalms that formed a kind of hymnbook of pilgrim praise used by Israelites as they travelled up to Jerusalem for the various festivals each year.[2] We see such journeys, for instance, in 1 Samuel 1, where Elkanah and Hannah go up year by year to the tabernacle of the LORD to worship, and in Luke 2 we read about Mary and Joseph going up with Jesus, aged about twelve, to the temple for the Passover. When they were journeying home, all together as part of that pilgrim band, it was some time before they realized Jesus was not there (they thought He was among the other pilgrims but He was left behind in the temple). You can imagine such a group of travelling pilgrims singing as they went along, or, perhaps as they stopped in the evenings to make camp, eating

---

1.   Psalms 120-134.

2.   Deuteronomy 16 outlines the three great festivals of Passover (Unleavened Bread), Pentecost (Weeks), and Tabernacles (Booths) where all able Israelite men were to make pilgrimage to the house of the LORD.

together and sharing in a time of prayer and praise. Certainly, as you read through these Psalms, you cannot miss the focus on Jerusalem, on Zion, and on travelling towards the city of God.

Real help for life's journeying

Such times of partings and journeying – whether ancient, or in our contemporary experience – can bring into sharp focus realities people tend to keep hidden much of the time, that, deep down, all of us know that life is full of uncertainties, and hazards, and potential dangers. There are fears all of us have which often rise to the surface at such times. They are real fears, and make us conscious that we need help on our journey, on our pilgrimage through this mortal coil. And this raises the question: Where does *your* help come from?

Here in this Psalm of pilgrimage, we have an honest appraisal of life in this world with all its hazards and threats, and we also have a clear answer to that question of where true help is to be found. It teaches us three very clear things: first, that life *is* full of hills; but that, second, there is a God who *made* the hills; and thirdly, that this God has a name. And this then raises a question for each of us.

A Real Problem

First, the Psalmist addresses a real Problem: Life *is* full of hills, and therefore *we are all looking for help*, as he opens by saying 'I lift my eyes to the hills. From where does my help come?' (1).

Many of us may need to rethink what may be our instinctive understanding of these lines. Scots, like me, tend to have an inborn love for the hills. Every time I fly back into Glasgow Airport, I love to sit on the right-hand side of the plane, and look out over the Campsie hills, and if it is a clear day – a rare occasion! – you might see further, up to Ben Lomond and beyond. If you are coming across the Atlantic it is even more spectacular: coming from the west, if you sit on the left side of the plane, you can look north, up the west coast of Scotland.

On a clear winter day you will see right up to the snow on the hills of Glencoe, perhaps right across to the Cairngorms, and seeing those hills does your heart good! When I lived in London, one of the things I found dispiriting was the flatness. (People used to talk about such and such a hill and I would look around and think, 'Where's this hill?' and I'd realize I had just walked up it without noticing.) They don't have any proper hills at all, and I used to long to see the bonny hills of Scotland! But, if you love the hills like that, it is easy to read this Psalm as though verse 1 is expressing a kind of longing for the hills. Some sung versions of the Psalm reinforce that 'Unto the hills around me I lift up my *longing* eyes'.[3]

Hills of fear and foreboding

But I am afraid that that is a misunderstanding of this verse. It is not a wistful longing that the Psalmist is expressing; it is a cry of fear and of foreboding because, for the Psalmist, the hills represent a real problem. This is not a longing look down from an aeroplane at the sun on beautiful hills; it is much more like a hillwalker in the mountains, with many miles still to walk to get back to his car, looking up and seeing very dark clouds coming at him over the hills, bringing freezing rain and threatening real danger in a very inhospitable place. Or, even more starkly, it is the kind of response a friend of mine encountered when visiting Nigeria some years ago, and was staying near some wonderful looking hills. When he said to his hosts, 'I'd love to go for a walk up in those hills' they looked back at him with horror in their eyes and said, 'No, no, not the *hills!*' When, puzzled, he asked why not, the reply was stark: 'the hills are full of snakes; and if the snakes do not kill you, they are full of bandits who will kill you.'

That is the thought in verse 1 of this Psalm. Remember, it is a song of Ascents; the pilgrims are journeying to Jerusalem,

---

3. Metrical Version of Psalm 121 by J D S Campbell (1845-1914), 121B in *Praise!* (Darlington: Praise Trust, 2000) (emphasis added).

walking through a very barren, hilly wilderness. These hills represented many dangers, so looking at the hills filled your heart with fear and concern. Just think of Jesus' story of the Good Samaritan; it was travelling that road between Jerusalem and Jericho that the traveller was set upon by bandits (Luke 10:29-30). The hills are not the pilgrim's friend, but his potential enemy; they are a real problem. In many ways the journey of pilgrims to Jerusalem *was* an acted parable of the whole life of faith – journeying towards the city of God, and to His presence and His joy. They understood that, for them – just as for us – the whole of their life was full of hills, with many fears, many dangers, much foreboding. 'I lift up my eyes', and what do I see? Hills all around! Potential danger, trouble, fears everywhere. That is why he asks the question immediately: where then am I going to find help?

This Psalm is full of realism about the problems of life. God's people are not immune from the hills. Believers face all the same kinds of struggles, all the same fears, all the same concerns, all the same potential hazards as everybody else. This is what verse 1 is saying. Of course there are some so-called Christian groups who want to deny this, claiming that life *can* be free from all these things, that real faith means a life of health and wealth and prosperity, that no hills will face *your* pilgrimage. But the Bible is much more realistic. It faces up to the problem squarely – *life is full of hills*.

The saints in the Old Testament, like the Psalmist, knew this very well, and it is expressed in so many other Psalms also. It is quite mistaken to think that the Old Testament is taken up only with the concerns of physical blessings and rewards, whereas the New Testament focuses more on spiritual things. It is plain here that the Psalmist is speaking figuratively about much more than just a physical journey to Jerusalem; he is clearly speaking about the whole of life, as verse 8 makes very obvious: 'The LORD will keep your going out and your coming in from this time forth and forevermore'. He's talking about all future life, not just now, but *forever*. And life now for the believer, as for everybody else, is full of hills – full of potential threats, harm, danger, and fears. We are all in the same boat, as human beings. Therefore we are all looking for help: 'From where does my help come?'

Well, where does *our* help come from? I guess for the average person that answer lies in many places. Often it is in *self-help*: looking to our careers or to our money for security; or perhaps to meditation, yoga, the latest diet, the latest fitness regime, a personal trainer, or many other things people turn to for help navigating the stresses and strains of life. It can be in *escapism*, hiding from the threats in the hills of life. Sometimes people desperately feel the need to hide, and they seek escape through drugs or alcohol, or some other consuming passion. Of course it can be in *religion* that people seek help. Whatever some new atheists might like to think, we are not living in a post-religious age; man-made philosophies and religions abound today, more than ever before, both conventional and unconventional, attracting many followers.

But the Christian, the believer in the God of Scripture, knows that help – real help – comes from only one place. That is the radical difference between someone who is a Christian and every other person in this world, religious or irreligious. We all face exactly the same hills in life but only the Christian believer has the answer that this Psalm gives.

A Real Power

The Christian faces these real problems with a real power. He knows that there is *a God who made* the hills and that *He* is the only possible source of real help.

This is what the rest of this Psalm is about – the Creator God, the maker of heaven and earth, the God who made the whole cosmos and is sovereign over even the hills of fear and foreboding, over every danger, toil and snare, everything we might ever confront in this life. The believer's answer to the issue of life is quite clear: *my* help comes from *this* God. People are looking everywhere for help in this world, but who or what in this world has the real power to give that help? Who can control and change the world on the scale that we really need? Only this world's Creator.

I remember years ago watching a television documentary about what was, then, the largest skyscraper in the world, being built in the Middle East. It followed right through the construction, and towards the end there was an interview with the architect who had overseen the whole project. The questioner asked him, 'What are you going to do now that you are moving on to other things?' He said, 'Well, I will be moving on *but* I'll be involved with this building for the whole of the rest of my life.' Why? 'Because when problems arise,' he said 'they'll need to come to me; I first envisaged this structure in my mind, I designed it in the plans, I oversaw the building of it – I am this building's creator, so I am the one who really knows the answers.' All human philosophies, ideas, religions and idols, along with our own powers, are *within* this world, this created order. We are bounded by it: created things. We are on the same level as the 'hills' (all the issues and the problems that we face.) Nothing *inside* this world can possibly help us with this world's problems. Only the God outside it all – the God who *made* the hills, the God who *controls* all of these mountainous issues in our lives – only He can possibly help us. But this God, the Creator of heaven and earth, *is* the helper of the Christian believer.

Notice that there is nothing vague about the help that is promised. To have *this* God as your helper means at least three things.

Ceaseless Guidance

First, verses 3-4 declare that it means having ceaseless guidance through all the paths of life:

> He will not let your foot be moved;
> he who keeps you will not slumber.

> Behold, he who keeps Israel
>   will neither slumber nor sleep.

It might be that the first line of verse 3 should be framed as a question: 'Will he really let your foot slip?' And the answer is decisive: your foot will *not* slip, it will *not* be moved, because you, personally, have the tireless attention of the God who made and controls the entire universe surrounding *you* (the pronoun is singular). He is always watching, He is always listening, He is always caring for *you*; He does not sleep. He does not even slumber. In other words, He is never even half asleep. He will never answer your cry and then fall back to sleep and forget ever to do anything about it. I am able to be not *asleep*, yet fully in 'slumber', especially early in the morning. In this state, my wife can ask me to do something and I will easily reply 'yes, no problem'. Early on in our marriage, she thought this was a good strategy! Quickly, however, she learned that my 'yes' did not mean 'yes'; when later in the day she asked if I had done as she had asked, I would say, 'What did you ask?' I could have a perfectly rational conversation, apparently, but would immediately forget all about it, because, though not actually sleeping, I was slumbering. But this God never slumbers, far less sleeps. He always hears and *does* everything that He promises. And He promises ceaseless guidance for the feet of those who are his: 'He will not let your foot be moved'.

What does that mean? It means that your own natural weakness and folly will not derail you in life if this is your God. A pilgrim on the path will of course often put their foot in the wrong place. They may perhaps take a foolish risk. They will certainly at times grow weary and perhaps lose their way. The same is true of all of us in life all the time. Believers like us are often foolish, aren't we? We also get weary, and we are regularly in danger of slipping very badly indeed. But He will *not* let your foot slip so as to let you fall to ultimate harm. That is God's promise – and it is such a liberating thing for us to know!

Liberation from fear, for fruitfulness

It liberates us from fear. Some Christians live in fear of putting their foot in the wrong place with God, of making a 'wrong turning' – a mistaken decision that will lead them into disaster, that will take them 'out of God's will' – and ruining everything of their future with God. But no, He will not let your foot slip like that! That is impossible if this is your God. This is no excuse for disobedience to God's Word in Scripture, of course- not ever. But it *is* an assurance that if you *are* trusting God, if you are walking in obedience to Him, if you are honestly seeking to follow the LORD Jesus Christ, He will not let you go, and you can be liberated from that fear.

It also liberates us for real fruitfulness – to have confident and venturesome faith because we know that we *have* God's ceaseless guidance. We do not need to be paralysed, waiting always for some special intervention by God, for some special 'guidance', or some special feeling of assurance before we will act or make a decision. No, we can know that He is constantly watching over us, that He is constantly guiding our feet on the path, and so we can know that peace and that assurance all the time. We have got to walk, of course; God is not going to do our walking for us. We have to step out and get on with things; but God will keep our feet secure. 'Why, even the hairs of your head are all numbered. Fear not' says Jesus Himself, and that is a great liberation.

Following the Reformation in the sixteenth century, the open proclamation of the Bible led people to a renewed discovery of the real sovereignty of God, giving believers the confidence to launch out in faith, trusting God to *be* their strength and their stay; it gave them this liberty to go out in faith, bringing the good news of Jesus Christ all over Europe, starting churches everywhere, despite much persecution. They knew that they did not have to wait for God to say 'Go!' in some special new revelation; instead, they knew that that their God was with them, promising to be their ceaseless guide in all they did. And if this God is *your* help, you also can be confident of His ceaseless guidance in all the paths of your life, too.

Sure Protection

But more than that, verses 5-6 promise that this God will be a sure protection in all the trials of life:

> The LORD is your keeper;
>> the LORD is your shade on your right hand.
> The sun shall not strike you by day,
>> nor the moon by night.

What the Psalmist is saying is that the natural scourges of life – which we must face alongside all humanity – will never overcome you if this God is your God; you have the constant protection of the God who created the whole natural world.

Again, this does not promise immunity from all these things; the Psalmist does not think that the sun's heat is somehow banished, so that Christians going to the beach on holiday need not wear any sun protection! Nor is he saying that the darkness may not bring fears to you, just as to others. But what he *is* saying is that he knows that there is a sure protection from this God in the midst of all these trials, for all of God's people. That is the constant refrain of the Bible. The LORD says to His beleaguered people, through Isaiah the prophet:

> "Fear not, for I have redeemed you;
>> I have called you by name, you are mine.
> When you pass through the waters, I will be with you;
>> and through the rivers, they shall not overwhelm you;
>> when you walk through fire you shall not be burned,
>> and the flame shall not consume you.

> (Isa. 43:1-2)

The apostle Peter speaks similarly of how believers are being 'shielded by God's power until the coming of the salvation that is ready to be revealed' when Jesus returns, and therefore amid 'all kinds of trials' – which *will* come and we *will* face – we can 'greatly rejoice' because we have this knowledge.[4] Paul, likewise, says that not by *avoiding* such things, but, '*in* all these things we are more than conquerors through him who loved us',[5] because this God watches over us, because we have a sure protection in all the trials of life. He is there 'on your right hand', close with you. Hi is far nearer to you than any of the threats in those hills. When the heat is on, *He* is your shade and your shelter. When things are dark, when fears abound, *He* is right there - He who made the entire universe.

What a difference that makes when the natural scourges of life bear down on us – as they *will* do in our lives. I remember speaking with a Christian lady in our church when she had just had a diagnosis of cancer, and was facing surgery. She was wonderfully at peace as she repeated these very words: 'The LORD is your keeper'. Some years ago a minister friend told me about one of the elders in his church who had a rare kind of blood cancer. The doctors had to remove and store some of his own bone marrow stem cells so that they could give him toxic chemotherapy that would knock out all of his marrow in order to get rid of all of the cancer cells. Following this, having kept the saved marrow stem cells safe in the freezer, they would bring it back and 'rescue' him by putting this back into his body to generate new blood cells. But, for some inexplicable reason, the freezer storing his stem cells had defrosted. The marrow that was to be put back into his body, upon which his whole life depended, was lost. It was certain, therefore, that he would die. Instead of being angry, or threatening the hospital with lawsuits, he simply bore witness. He said to his doctor, 'I am a Christian believer and I trust that my LORD Jesus is the Sovereign Creator in whose hands are all of these things, and so I am at peace.' I remember, too, after my own father had a major stroke, sitting with my mother at breakfast, the day

4. 1 Peter 1:5-6, NIV.
5. Romans 8:37.

after; I will never forget her praying, and thanking God for 'His good, pleasing and perfect will'.[6] She, like the Psalmist, knew that we have in this God a sure and Sovereign Protector in all the natural trials of life.

I do not know what you may be facing in your life just now. Perhaps it is the scorching sun of illness or sorrow or family worries, or it may be the deadly fears of night when, in those dark and quiet moments, you ruminate on all kinds of looming uncertainties in life. But I do know that if this God is *your* God, then you have a promise of sure protection in *all* of these trials. The Lord is *your* shade and He will be at your right hand, there beside you in all of it.

Certain Promise

Furthermore, as verses 7-8 tell us, you also have a certain promise of unending life.

> The Lord will keep you from all evil;
> > he will keep your life.
> The Lord will keep your going out and your coming in
> > from this time forth and forevermore.

What that means is that even death itself cannot harm you if this God is *your* God. Your life is in the hands of the eternal God now, and from this time forth, and forevermore. Is that not an extraordinary promise?

As we get older, ill health and thoughts of death, and perhaps fear of the process of dying, can bring a great mountain of fear into our lives. For some, very sadly, that great enemy will arrive prematurely: a sudden illness in the family, or worse. We live in a world where violence, murder, and terrorism are a real threat. But even if we live a very sheltered life, all of us in the end must face the great evil the Bible calls 'the last enemy':

---

6. These words from Romans 12:2 were part of that day's reading from *Daily Light*, which we had just read together.

death.[7] Our mortality will cast an ever-greater shadow over us as life goes on; it gets harder to hide from as time passes, much as we may try. As Christian believers we are not immune from that; to dust we also will return. But this Psalm tells us that if this God is our God, even death, the last enemy, the ultimate evil, shall not overwhelm us. The LORD will keep you safe from 'all evil'; He will 'keep your life' now and forever. We are not immune from the physical evils of death, so as we do not experience them; but we will be armed against them so that they can never overwhelm us. We shall not fear the valley of the shadow of death because the LORD is with us even there (Ps. 23:4). Here is real resurrection hope, right in the heart of the Old Testament. The believer's life with this God will not cease; it goes on 'forevermore'. Though many things may afflict us, and indeed *will* afflict us, we have God's promise that no ultimate harm can ever befall us.

This is a wonderful promise, and it is one that we all need, because, as Jesus says to those who follow Him, 'even your parents and brothers, your relations and friends, will betray you. Some of you will be put to death; and all will hate you for your allegiance to me.' There is great *realism*; but the LORD also gives great *reassurance*: 'But not a hair of your head will be lost. By standing firm, you will win true life'.[8] The LORD *will* 'watch over your going out and your coming in from this time forth and forevermore.'

Some Christians do live their lives in inordinate fear. They worry, 'Will I endure, will I really be saved, can I be sure?' The answer of this Psalm is 'Yes! Trust Him, and He *will* keep you, now and always.' You may say, 'But what about my sins; I muck up so badly and so often?' Look at what verse 7 says, 'The LORD will *keep* you from *all* evil.' Not even your sins can get in the way of that promise. That is why 1 John 3:20 is perhaps my favourite verse in the whole Bible: 'whenever

7. 1 Corinthians 15:26.

8. Luke 21:16-19, NEB.

our heart condemns us, God is greater than our heart, and he knows everything.' You have a certain promise of unending eternal life if this is your God. He is, as Peter names Him, the God of all grace:

> The one great and glorious reality in a believer's experience is this: the God of all grace has called him, having predestined him before all worlds to share his eternal glory. When a man has faith in Christ for salvation it means that out of the mystery of eternity there has come a loving and mighty hand that lays hold upon his life, claiming it for an eternity of joy and blessedness, glorious beyond understanding and almost beyond belief. Now, cries Peter, 'set that over and against your trial, whatever it may be, however severe it may become, wherever it may touch you. There is no possible combination of adverse circumstances in which this glorious truth will not make all the difference.'[9]

If this God is your God, then a loving and mighty hand has laid hold upon you, both now and forevermore; you have a certain promise of eternal life.

A Real Person

The third and vital thing the Psalmist points us to is not just to a power, but to a real person. This God has a name – so we can find Him, and know His help.

The Psalm is not just talking vaguely about G-O-D – an unknown being, a distant Creator, an unknowable entity. This God has a personal name: 'My help comes from the LORD (1), there again in verses 5, 7, and 8. When you see the name LORD in capitals like that in our Bibles, it means *Yahweh*,

---

9.   James Philip, *1 Peter: Reading the Bible with James Philip* (Glasgow: Tron Media, 2014). James Philip's Bible Readings (on Psalms and all other Bible Books) are all available for free at the Tron Church website: https://www.tron.church/resources.

the name of the covenant God of Israel.[10] He, and He alone, is the God who made all things, the only God. He is the God of Abraham and Isaac and Jacob, the God of Moses, the God of David, the God of the Psalmists. He is the God who *reveals* Himself, which is the only way He can be truly known, but He has done so all through history to His people so that He can be known. He is the only Creator, and so He is the only Helper, the only Saviour. He 'who created the heavens, (he is God!), who formed the earth and made it... I am the LORD, and there is no other... a righteous God and a Saviour, there is none besides me'.[11] There is no pantheon, or hierarchy of gods, no other gods at all – He alone is God.

He is the God who revealed more and more of Himself all down the ages, speaking through the Law and the Prophets and the Psalmists until, in these last days, He has revealed Himself fully and ultimately in His Son, the LORD Jesus Christ. He it is who 'created the world' and who reveals ultimately to the world 'the radiance of the glory of God and the exact imprint of his nature'. He it is who 'upholds the universe by the word of his power.'[12] He is the one in whom Paul says 'all the fullness of God was pleased to dwell' in bodily form.[13] He is not the *false* god of Islam, or of Mormonism, or of Jehovah's Witnesses, or any others who deny the full deity of the LORD Jesus Christ; there is no help to be found there. But *this* God has a name, and He can be known. His whole purpose in creation is that He *will* be known – as the one who gives ceaseless guidance to all who love Him, as the one who gives sure protection to all who will take refuge in Him, as one who promises unending life to all who will trust in His promises.

---

10. See note 4 in Chapter 1.
11. Isaiah 45:18-21.
12. Hebrews 1:2-3.
13. Colossians 1:19.

No other name

The true God has a *name*. But He only has *one* name; He alone is God, there is no other. He has now in these last days made Himself fully known only through His Son, God incarnate, the LORD Jesus Christ. Therefore, He can be known only *one* way: by the name of Jesus Christ, the risen Saviour and LORD. It is the risen Jesus who has been highly exalted to receive the name that is above every other name, the name of LORD, God Himself. That is why the apostle Peter says, 'there is salvation in no one else, for there is no other name under heaven given among men by which we must be saved.'[14]

All human beings have a real problem: life is full of ominous *hills* and we all need help. But there is a real power: the *God* who *made* the hills, and He *is* the only hope of help. And that power is in a real person, because this God has a *name*, so we can know Him, and we can find all the help we need.

A Real Question

So this Psalm surely leaves us with a question: is this God *your* God? Where does *your* help come from?

I hope you know He is your God, because if He is not, then it means that none of this really is yours. You have no ceaseless guidance in all the paths of your life, only anxiety, fear, hesitation. There is no sure protection in all the trials of your life, only despair and sadness and bitterness. Nor do you have this certain promise of unending life, just uncertainty and foreboding and the chill fear of approaching death. If this God – made known to our world ultimately and forever in the LORD Jesus Christ – is *not* your God, then none of these things are yours, because they cannot be found anywhere else. There is *no other name* under heaven where you can find ultimate help, ultimate salvation.

---

14.   Acts 4:12.

But why should this God not be your God also? He *can* be your God; He *wants* to be your God. That is why the only true God, who is beyond and outside our world, came *into* the world: 'Turn to me and be saved, all the ends of the earth!' He says 'for I am God, there is no other' (Isa. 45:22). He came from the bright glory of heaven, into the dark danger of this world with all its fearsome hills. He came – the God who *made* the heavens and the earth – to be a lonely pilgrim, walking that road to Jerusalem, and to the cross, to give His life as a ransom for many – so that He might promise to all who love Him that He will be their Saviour, keeping their life 'from this time forth and forevermore.'

Where does *your* help come from? Is it from the name of the God made known in our Lᴏʀᴅ Jesus Christ?

It can be – because He is the God who says, 'Come to me, *all* who labour and are heavy-laden,' burdened by all the hills of this life; 'come to *me* and I will give you rest'.[15] And 'whoever comes to me, I will *never* cast out'.[16]

---

15. Matthew 11:28.

16. John 6:37

Joining the Choir of the King

Psalm 145 - a song of praise

A Song of Praise. Of David.

¹I will extol you, my God and King,
 and bless your name forever and ever.
² Every day I will bless you
 and praise your name forever and ever.
³ Great is the LORD, and greatly to be praised,
 and his greatness is unsearchable.

⁴ One generation shall commend your works to another,
 and shall declare your mighty acts.
⁵ On the glorious splendor of your majesty,
 and on your wondrous works, I will meditate.
⁶ They shall speak of the might of your awesome deeds,
 and I will declare your greatness.
⁷ They shall pour forth the fame of your abundant goodness
 and shall sing aloud of your righteousness.

⁸ The LORD is gracious and merciful,
 slow to anger and abounding in steadfast love.
⁹ The LORD is good to all,
 and his mercy is over all that he has made.

¹⁰ All your works shall give thanks to you, O LORD,

and all your saints shall bless you!
[11] They shall speak of the glory of your kingdom
        and tell of your power,
[12] to make known to the children of man your mighty deeds,
        and the glorious splendor of your kingdom.
[13] Your kingdom is an everlasting kingdom,
        and your dominion endures throughout all generations.

[The LORD is faithful in all his words
        and kind in all his works.]
[14] The LORD upholds all who are falling
        and raises up all who are bowed down.
[15] The eyes of all look to you,
        and you give them their food in due season.
[16] You open your hand;
        you satisfy the desire of every living thing.
[17] The LORD is righteous in all his ways
        and kind in all his works.
[18] The LORD is near to all who call on him,
        to all who call on him in truth.
[19] He fulfills the desire of those who fear him;
        he also hears their cry and saves them.
[20] The LORD preserves all who love him,
        but all the wicked he will destroy.

[21] My mouth will speak the praise of the LORD,
        and let all flesh bless his holy name forever and ever.
                                                    Psalm 145

When my wife and I first visited Italy some years ago, we found the sheer scale of history and beauty in places like Rome and Florence staggering. It almost made up for being charged seven euros for a coffee and nine euros for a glass of coke just because we sat down at a table instead of standing at the counter (which apparently is the trick to decimate the bill). For a Scotsman that was beyond the pale, but at least I did not pay £54 for an ice cream, like some poor tourists I read about in Venice!

Like most visitors to these places, we took some guided tours, and in doing so were struck by the sharp contrast between two of our guides. One day we had a very poor guide: her repertoire really amounted to little more than constant repetition of phrases like, 'Look, this is very interesting!' or 'Look, isn't this very beautiful!' As she went on like this, very quickly we were bored and just switched off. No doubt all these things *were* very beautiful and interesting, but she told us nothing to really open our eyes or pique our interest; she did not help us to see and appreciate the beauty and the wonder of them better for ourselves. By contrast, another day we had a guide who was quite different. Even before we reached the sights we were to visit, she had expounded to us the full story of these places and explained their significance. She painted such a rich picture for us that we were already saying spontaneously to ourselves, 'Isn't that extraordinary! That is staggering!' and when we did come to see these things, we were filled with wonder. Our 'praise' was spontaneous, because our hearts and minds had been given a reason to praise: not because we were being urged to praise something, but because we clearly sensed it as the only appropriate response.

It can be similar when we think about praising God. Perhaps you have read books or heard sermons exhorting you to praise more, or to pray more, because poverty in praise of God, and in prayer to God, is a cause of deeply lacking Christian experience. There is, of course, a lot of truth in that. But the problem is that this kind of exhortation just to praise God more, or to pray more, doesn't really seem to help, does it? It is like our guide *telling* us to be interested without actually *interesting* us at all. You cannot be just told to wonder and adore at something; you need to be led into wonder and adoration. However, a great deal of exhortation to praise in the Christian church can often do the very opposite; it seems to sink us into despair and a feeling of inadequacy. I have certainly felt that at times, if at some Christian meeting the person called the 'worship leader' says, 'Now let's make sure we really, really praise God in this song, and let's sing this song as though we really, really mean it!' You may have heard the same kind of thing. But whenever I hear that, I just find my heart sinking. In fact, sometimes I feel I want to sing a lament, not a song of praise, just to be contrary!

Vital praise

But praise is vital nevertheless. If you read on after this Psalm you will see that the last five Psalms in the Psalter (Psalms 146-150) each begin with a command to praise – 'Praise the Lord!' Likewise, the Bible is clear that not to be praising God is in fact a great sin. Deuteronomy 28:47 says that if Israel did 'not serve the Lord your God *with joyfulness and gladness of heart*' [emphasis added] they would be held accountable and judged by God. William Still, in his Bible notes on that verse, put it strikingly: this tells us that 'spontaneous praise is not the iced cake of Christian worship and service, but its mere bread and butter'.[1] To be people who live in joyful praise of the Lord is simply what it means to be people of true faith.

Now in response to speaking like this the cynic may say, 'What a selfish, unattractive God this Christian God is, who demands praise for Himself all the time!' C.S. Lewis used to say exactly that when he was an atheist. He used to think this way until he realised what is the most obvious fact about praise: that real *enjoyment* of something, or someone, must naturally overflow into *praise*.

The world rings with praise—lovers praising their mistresses, readers their favourite poet, walkers praising the countryside, players praising their favourite game— praise of weather, wines, dishes, actors, motors, horses,

---

1. William Still, *Congregational Record and Daily Bible Readings* (Aberdeen: Gilcomston South Church, August 1965), 19.

colleges, countries, historical personages, children, flowers, mountains, rare stamps, rare beetles, even sometimes politicians or scholars. I had not noticed how the humblest, and at the same time *most balanced and capacious minds*, praised *most*, while *the cranks, misfits, and malcontents* praised *least*. The good critics found something to praise in many imperfect works; the bad ones continually narrowed the list of books we might be allowed to read. The healthy and unaffected man, even if luxuriously brought up and widely experienced in good cookery, could praise a very modest meal: the dyspeptic and the snob found fault with all. Except where intolerably adverse circumstances interfere, *praise almost seems to be inner health made audible.*[2]

Real enjoyment naturally flows into praise. But more than that, it *needs* praise. The world rings with praise because praise is the *inevitable consummation* of true enjoyment:

We delight to praise what we enjoy because the praise not merely expresses but completes the enjoyment; it is its appointed consummation. It is not out of compliment that lovers keep on telling one another how beautiful they are; *the delight is incomplete till it is expressed.* It is frustrating to have discovered a new author and *not* to be able to tell anyone how good he is; to come suddenly, at the turn of the road, upon some mountain valley of unexpected grandeur and then to *have to keep silent* because the people with you care for it no more than for a tin can in the ditch; to hear a good joke and find *no one to share it with...*[3]

---

2. C. S. Lewis, *Reflection on the Psalms* (Glasgow: Collins, 1961), 80, emphasis mine.

3. C.S. Lewis, *Psalms*, 81, emphasis mine.

We all know that sense of enjoyment necessitating praise. We come back from a wonderful holiday, or a great rugby match, or a camp, or a day on the hills – or whatever it is – and we talk about it, we show our friends the photographs, we describe it: we *praise* what we have experienced. If we never did that, the experience itself would actually be diminished.

The inner health of praise

And so it is with our praise of God. C.S. Lewis goes on to quote the first question of The Westminster Shorter Catechism (a helpful summary of biblical teaching) which tells us that 'man's chief end', or purpose, is 'to *glorify* God and *enjoy* him forever', and he points out that 'these are the same thing. Fully to enjoy is to glorify. In commanding us to glorify Him, God is inviting us to enjoy Him.'[4] To fully enjoy *is* to glorify; it is to *praise*. Praise is *inner health made audible*, and our praise of God therefore expresses the reality about the most important thing of all: the inner health of our relationship with God.

So the key question is: how can we be led into, and nourished in, that inner health of experience and enjoyment of God, which expresses itself in real and spontaneous praise?

I want to suggest that Psalm 145 gives us an ABC of this life of inner health. It is quite literally an ABC, because the Psalm is what we call an acrostic: each verse begins with succeeding letters of the Hebrew alphabet, a device probably to help memorization of its message. It is a deliberately memorable lesson, taught and led by King David, the sweet singer of Israel. He is the one who is leading all his people together in praise, and verse 1 begins with a king praising a far greater King: 'I will extol you, *my* God and King.'

A Sovereign praising The Sovereign

Perhaps you can remember watching a great State occasion on television, such as a Royal wedding or State funeral.

---

4. C.S. Lewis, *Psalms*, 82.

I remember watching one of these taking place in Westminster Abbey and being struck by the position of our former Queen, Elizabeth II. Normally during her lifetime, of course, she was the centre of attention. Yet in that vast building she looked so very small. There she was, seated prominently at the front, yes, but surrounded by all the congregation, and with them addressing *her* praise to *her* God and King: a sovereign praising a far greater Sovereign. Christians were rightly thankful for her example, and likewise for her Christmas broadcasts, which were often far more clear and boldly Christian in their message than those of the anemic ecclesiastical leaders in the West today. So often in life the late Queen humbly pointed her whole nation and commonwealth to her true Sovereign, the LORD Jesus Christ; she did so likewise in death. Her Majesty's chosen hymn began her State funeral pointing upwards, proclaiming 'So be it, LORD; *thy throne* shall never, like earth's proud empires, pass away', and it ended by pointing forwards, to the new creation where, Queen though she was, she rejoiced to cast her crown 'before thee, lost in wonder, love and praise!'[5]

And so it is here. David is Israel's great king, the LORD's Anointed, and yet he knows that he has a far greater LORD and King, the LORD his God. David's praise points above, to God's throne in heaven. But he also pointed his people forward, to God's coming to earth in history; David himself foreshadowed a far greater King, great David's greater Son, The Anointed One, the LORD Jesus Christ. Ultimately it is He of whom these words speak most fully and truly, as Hebrews 2 makes clear by quoting David (from Psalm 22) and telling us that it is great David's greater Son, Jesus, who cries out, 'In the midst of the congregation *I* will sing your praise'[6] [emphasis added]. God's true King, risen and ascended to glory, is now leading all the true congregation of His people

---

5. The opening hymn was *'The day thou gavest, LORD, is ended'* by John Ellerton (1826-93), and the closing hymn, *'Love divine, all loves excelling'*, by Charles Wesley (1707-88) (emphasis added).

6. Hebrews 2:12.

in praise of God His Father and *their* Father, His God and *their* God. 'Every day I will bless you and praise your name *forever and ever*' [emphasis added], says David here in verse 2, anticipating that far greater fulfilment.

Awakening praise

So what does God's King, as our praise guide, say to us to create in us the desire, and the ability, to join in the praise of our great God and King? How does he bring us to spontaneous praise, to join the choir of those who will glorify Him and so truly enjoy Him forever?

The answer is simply that he opens our eyes and our ears to understand what verse 12 of Psalm 145 calls 'the glorious splendour of [his] kingdom'. In other words, he awakens our hearts to the extraordinary good news in the gospel of the everlasting kingdom of God. This Psalm points us to a God who is a *King of unsearchable greatness* and to the promises He makes to those who will be His people, in a *covenant of unchangeable faithfulness*. Whether in 'the former days' of David and his people awaiting Christ's first coming, or for us in these 'last days' in which we live waiting for Christ's return, it is only as God's people really grasp and understand these wonderful truths that they will freely and spontaneously join in the *choir of unquenchable witness* to the great King.[7] Thus blessing the name of the LORD, as we proclaim the glory of His King, telling the

---

7.   Former and latter/last days is a way the New Testament refers to the era either side of the coming of Jesus Christ in history, and His resurrection to glory. Paul reminds the Christian church just how vital all the Old Testament Scriptures from these '*former days*' are for us, written as they are 'for our instruction' so that 'through the encouragement of the Scriptures we might have hope' (Rom. 15:4), despite the fact that 'in these *last days* he has spoken to us by his Son' (Heb. 1:1). We now have, in the New Testament, the ultimate revelation of God in the words and work of Jesus, but there has only ever been *one* people of God, in Christ by faith, going right back to the earliest of the patriarchs. That is why the saints of the former days stand as the examples of true faith for Christians in the latter days, for both the apostle Paul (e.g. in Rom. 4) and in Hebrews 11. There has only ever been, as the hymn says, 'one church, one faith, one LORD.'

world of the glories of His eternal kingdom, is the very heart of real Christian praise.[8]

Let's look at this Psalm a little more closely. Verses 1 and 21 are like bookends at the beginning and end of Psalm 145: the king declaring that he will bless the name of the LORD forever. Then, the centrepiece of the Psalm in verses 10-13a focuses on *all* the saints likewise blessing His name, proclaiming His glorious kingdom to the world forever. And on either side of those central verses, which are like a pivot point, our guide shows us why they are joining him in doing that.

A King of Unsearchable Greatness

From verse 3 to the first half of verse 13 the Psalmist shows forth our God as a King of *unsearchable greatness*: 'Great is the LORD, and greatly to be praised, and his greatness is unsearchable' (3). Our God is a Sovereign Ruler whose greatness is revealed in works of superabundant goodness and grace.

The message all through these verses is simple - God is great! But what does that mean? To say "God is great!' can certainly mean very different things today. Indeed, this phrase has come to have a chilling, fearful quality, for many: for example when a crowd is heard chanting 'Allahu Akbar!' – 'God is great!'. That is the cry of the Islamic jihadi as he is about to blow himself up trying to maim and kill hundreds of women and children. There *is* a kind of greatness that conveys something terrible, and frightening. When you see some of the vast buildings and palaces belonging to great rulers and empires of the past, you sense the greatness of raw power. You see it in the ruins of imperial Rome, in the sheer scale of the Colosseum; it is breathtaking. And when you start to imagine the greatness of the bloody spectacles that took place there, the merciless brutality that went on at the whim of the Caesars, you tremble at the raw power of that kind of greatness.

---

8. Hebrews 13:15

Is that what we mean when we say our God is *great*?

There is a right sense in which we rightly fear and tremble at the greatness of God; the Bible tells us He is a God to be feared, treated seriously with reverence and awe, not to be trifled with or to be taken for granted. This 'fear of the Lord' is the very beginning of wisdom and knowledge, and the key to life, says the book of Proverbs.[9] But the focus of the Psalmist here is rather different. We are led to praise a greatness that is manifest above all in all the works of God, and His works are works of unsearchable *goodness* and extraordinary *grace*. Verses 4-6 are replete with God's great and wonderful works, His interventions in the lives of His people: 'One generation shall commend your works to another, and shall declare your mighty acts (4). 'The glorious splendour' of God's majesty is revealed *in* His 'wondrous works' (5). It is His 'awesome deeds' that declare His greatness (6).

Great goodness, mercy, and love

David is speaking very personally here: '*I* will declare your greatness' [emphasis added]. It is exactly the language he uses in 2 Samuel 7:21 to describe everything God has done for him and his family, just as He had promised: calling him out of the fields and making him a king and a ruler over his people, promising his progeny would sit enthroned on that throne for ever. He says there, 'because of your promise, and according to your own heart, you have brought about all this *greatness*' [emphasis added]. God's greatness is known in what He does for His people, and all He does is full of 'abundant goodness' and 'righteousness' (7). This word 'righteousness' sometimes is translated 'deliverance', because God's righteousness is His way of putting things to *right* by righting all wrongs.[10]

---

9.   Proverbs 1:7; 2:5; 9:10; 10:27; 14:27; 19:23; 28:14; 29:25.

10.   See, for example, Psalm 40:9-10, ESV.

Verses 8-9 further describe the greatness of the God of the Bible as above all a greatness in *love* and *mercy* towards all He has made.

> The LORD is gracious and merciful,
>> slow to anger and abounding in steadfast love.
> The LORD is good to all,
>> and his mercy is over all that he has made.

Our God is gracious and merciful, slow to anger, abounding in steadfast love. The Psalm here is quoting from Exodus 34:6, where at Sinai God appeared to Moses in the greatest self-revelation of God in the Old Testament. As Moses was hidden in the cleft of the rock, the LORD passed by Moses and revealed His name to him: The LORD, the name that reveals His unsearchable divine greatness as a greatness of goodness and grace, of mercy and compassion, and of longsuffering love.[11]

We should not miss that these words from Exodus 34 are some of the most frequently quoted words in the rest of the Old Testament, because they sing aloud of the kind of greatness that sinful human beings most *need* of deity – mercy and grace. This is the greatness we find in our God, the God of Scripture. The prophet Jonah quotes those words back to God, in a very disapproving way, because God had shown Himself to be exactly that, gracious and merciful to that pagan city that had repented.[12] Indeed, as Derek Kidner points out, that incident proves verse 9 of the Psalm true, because God's mercy in Nineveh extended not just to people, but even to the city's many cattle:[13] 'The LORD is good to *all*... that he has made'.

By the way, this gives the lie to nonsense spoken by some environmentalists who want to pin the blame for all exploitation

---

11. Most English Bibles translate as LORD in capital letters the Hebrew letters YHWH, which is the revealed covenant name of the God of Israel. See note 4, Chapter 1.

12. Jonah 4:2, 11.

13. Kidner, *Psalms 73-150*, 481.

of the planet on the Bible's influence, and the Christian God – as if God's command to man to rule over the earth for Him was a command to *disregard* His precious creation, to mutilate it, to disfigure it! Of course, it was exactly the opposite: God made man to rule over the world in *His* image, with *His* compassionate care, for *all* that He has made. It is man who, in *casting off* God's yoke, has scourged the world with a hideously disfigured image of selfish, corrupted humanity. By contrast, The LORD is good, 'and his mercy is over all that he has made.' Read the fourth commandment: in the liberated rhythms of life commanded among God's redeemed people there is a Sabbath rest not only for His people of faith, but for every servant, every sojourner – even for the ox and the ass and the rest of the livestock.[14] Our God is good and compassionate, His mercy is over *all* that He has made.

Our God is a King of unsearchable greatness and goodness: an absolute Sovereign, indeed, but one whose greatness is revealed in the superabundant works of goodness and grace, a goodness which, when we come to see it, is simply overwhelming.

Amazing grace

That is certainly the impression conveyed by this Psalmist king's words as he points us to his God and true King. His words of personal praise pour out as he thinks about all that God has done in *his* life, and he joins his own praise with the praise of many generations of those who likewise have seen God at work in their lives. That is what happens when we, too, begin to meditate on the goodness and grace of God's works in our own lives, as we find is expressed in so many of

---

14. Exodus 4:8-11. Of course, the Bible never confuses mankind with animals; It is man whom he 'has crowned with glory and honour' and given 'dominion over' all creation, putting all the animal kingdom 'under his feet', (Ps. 8:5-9). Scripture is very clear that the earth, and everything in it is created for mankind, to serve mankind, not vice versa. Human beings are not to be sacrificed in order to serve 'mother earth', as the idolatries of neo-pagan 'green' ideologies today promote.

the great hymns of praise in the Christian church. 'O to grace how great a debtor daily *I'm* constrained to be' wrote Robert Robinson, in the hymn 'Come thou fount of every blessing'. John Newton, the formerly brutal slave trader, sang of God's *amazing grace* to him personally, such that '*I* once was lost but now am found, was blind but now *I* see'. Likewise, the African pastor Emmanuel Sibomana penned the wonderful hymn 'O how the grace of God amazes *me!*' in his apprehension of Christ's wonderful gospel[15] [emphasis added].

If we stop for a moment and think back over our own lives, surely every believer can bear testimony to the greatness of goodness we have experienced at God's hand. I certainly can, as can the church where I serve, even when we look back together at some very dark, painful times we had to go through as a family of faith. We can see that we are still able to testify to the wonderful goodness of God, to the awesome deeds that He has done for us, and among us. We are witnesses to His gracious provision in those times, and of the way He led us through them, the way He miraculously erased bitterness from our minds and hearts and gave us joy in our heart, and the way that, even in the hardest times, He continued to save people and add them to our congregation – all wonderful reasons for us to praise His unsearchable greatness. So my own testimony, and our church's testimony is that we can certainly sing with Fanny Crosby:

All the way my Saviour leads me,
cheers each winding path I tread,
gives me grace for every trial,
feeds me with the Living Bread.[16]

The God who leads us in the path of life with such kindness is a King of unsearchable greatness.

---

15.   This hymn was the inspiration for Sinclair B Ferguson's book *By Grace Alone*. It is a great hymn, but little sung today, and well worthy of rediscovery. It can be found in the hymnbook *Praise!*, No 749.

16.   Frances J Van Alstyne (Fanny Crosby), 1820-1915.

A Covenant of Unchangeable Faithfulness

Verses 13b-20 reminds us of something else which will draw us into joyful praise: our *gospel* is a covenant of *unchangeable faithfulness*.

'The Lord is faithful in all his words
and kind *[unchangeably loyal]* in all his works' (13).[17]

The Psalmist is saying that our God is a saving Redeemer whose covenant is marked by *His* faithfulness and righteousness: what *He* says, He does; what *He* promises, He will always fulfil. He is faithfully righteous and righteously faithful – unchangeably loyal in all His covenant promises to all the world, but also in a very special way to those who are His own.

God's restraining faithfulness towards the world

Verses 14-17 speak of God's covenant of restraining faithfulness for the whole world, His promise to preserve the world and to restrain evil:

The Lord upholds *all* who are falling
and raises up *all* who are bowed down.
The eyes of *all* look to you,
and you give them their food in due season.
You open your hand;
you satisfy the desire of *every* living thing.
The Lord is righteous in *all* [emphasis added] his ways
and kind in *all* his works [emphasis added].

---

17.   Not all Hebrew manuscripts include these two lines; however, they do appear in various versions, including the Greek Old Testament (LXX). Virtually the same statement is repeated in verse 17, the only difference being 'righteous ways' replaces 'faithful words'. The word translated by ESV as 'kind' in both verses 'might be better rendered 'loyal' or (NEB) 'unchanging'. Kidner, *Psalms 73-150*, 482. C.f. Jeremiah 3:12 (NIV) where '"I am *faithful*," declares the Lord' in contrast to '*faithless* Israel' [emphasis added].

Sometimes we may think that if God is great and merciful, how then can there still be so much evil in the world? How can there be so much wrong, and tragedy, so much sickness and death if God is so great and so good? The answer to that lies not at God's door but at man's; it is humans who are the anarchists in this world, the architects of this world's disasters, not God. Man rebelled against the good and gracious rule of God; Genesis 3 describes the tragic beginning and Romans 1 spells out the calamitous consequences for us. Human beings have dishonoured God, having become futile in their thinking and darkened in their hearts, and because of this, thrice we are told 'God gave them up'. He has left people to their own devices – given them up to debasement in heart, in mind, and even in body.[18] It is we who have done with this world what *we* want to do, not what God commanded us to do. The mess and the misery of this world lies squarely at the door of mankind.

Human depravity

It is easy for us to forget just how deep that depravity can be. Recently I was reading an account about the times of the Second World War; in doing so, just to have to grapple with the atrocities of the Nazi Reich, all that went on under that regime of utter darkness and wickedness, was sickening. We want to write off these terrible things as aberrations, and yet the truth is that the heart of man has not changed, nor the dreadful evils which, as Jesus said, come 'from within, out of the heart of man' to defile life so horrifically.[19] Our exposure to instant world news today surely magnifies this to us: as we hear about awful machine-gun massacres in American schools by disaffected youngsters becoming so warped in their thinking; of terrorist suicide bombings in many places; of gangs of men in the UK trafficking teenage girls as sex-slaves, and countless other horrors. What often shocks people the most is when

---

18. Romans 1:24-28.
19. Mark 7:21.

such things come to light right in the middle of the quiet towns and suburban areas where they live. These things are not just far away in 'another kind of place'; they are all too close for comfort.

Judgment delayed

The real miracle is that, despite all this, God has *not* yet executed total and final judgment on this warped and wicked planet. We should be eternally thankful for this. We need to remember that when sometimes we are longing for God to end all the suffering and evil and wrongdoing, when we say, 'Lord, won't you bring an end to all these terrible things!' But what are we asking God when we pray that? It is to ask for God's final judgment, for complete and real retribution for all sin, all offence against God – *including* our own. Do not be mistaken, that day will come. Peter tells us so very clearly in his second letter: 'the day of judgment and destruction of the ungodly', as he calls it.[20] God is not slow, in doing justly to punish evil, says Peter, but He is patient. Not wishing that any should perish, He is still, in His great mercy, keeping the world, preserving it until that day.[21] He is restraining man's worst evil, so that we as human beings, with all our self-destructive impulses, cannot utterly self-destruct and take this whole planet with us. God has been, and still is, unchangeably faithful to His covenant promise to do that.

Common grace

That was His covenant way back in ancient times, with Noah: 'Never again shall there be a flood to utterly destroy the earth' says the Lord.[22] God will not allow man's evil to become so utterly unrestrained that it *will* destroy this world. No, in His mercy He is restraining evil, keeping it on a leash, and blessing

---

20. 2 Peter 3:7.
21. 2 Peter 3:9.
22. Genesis 9:11.

this world, in spite of all its sin, rebellion, and rejection of Him. Our heavenly Father is a God who 'makes his sun rise on the evil and on the good, and sends rain on the just and on the unjust' says Jesus.[23] This is what verses 14-16 are speaking about. It is what is sometimes called God's *common grace* to all creation. He feeds and clothes, and He gives the joy and the laughter of family and of friendship, He gives fulfilment in life with abundant generosity to human beings – even to those who hate Him. Every day of life on this planet, for every creature, is a day of the abundant blessing of God's grace; every day is owed to His unchangeably faithful word of covenant promise to this world.

God's redeeming faithfulness towards His own

But even this wonderful truth does not exhaust God's faithfulness. In verses 18-20 the Psalmist spells this out wonderfully:

> The LORD is near to all who call on him,
>   to all who call on him in truth.
> He fulfills the desire of those who fear him;
>   he also hears their cry and saves them.
> The LORD preserves all who love him,
>   but all the wicked he will destroy.

God's righteousness means not just a *restraining* faithfulness towards all the world, but a *redeeming* faithfulness towards all who are His own. His covenant promise is to be present with His people in a unique way, and to rescue all who are His own, for all eternity. Indeed, this is the underlying purpose of God's preservation of this whole world, restraining evil and not allowing it to be destroyed. All this is to give time and opportunity for His greatest grace and mercy of all: His saving covenant of redemption – first given to Abraham – to call out for His very own a people who would be His for ever,

---

23. Matthew 5:45.

through the Seed of promise, made known at last in great David's greater Son, our LORD Jesus Christ.

Judgment will come

From the beginning to the end of the book of Psalms – indeed of the whole Bible – it is clear that an ultimate division of all humanity will be made at the end of time. Psalm 1 opens the Psalter with an absolute contrast: the way of the *righteous* and the way of the *wicked*. There is a refuge for the righteous forever, beyond death, 'for the LORD knows the way of the righteous'; but equally 'the way of the wicked will perish'.[24] There is a judgment day to come. God is faithful to His covenant of restraint, but only until all is fulfilled, then there *will* be that final judgment. There is nothing in all the teaching of the LORD Jesus Christ that is plainer on His lips than this absolute certainty. It is just as plain here in Psalm 145: 'all the wicked he will destroy' (20).

Even if you are reading this as a Christian, you may find this difficult to come to terms with. Certainly, many people today are outraged even to consider such a thing – that 'all the wicked [God] will destroy'. There is a strange irony here, because if you ask such a person, 'is the reason you don't like it because *you* are wicked?' they are likely to be even more outraged: 'How dare you call me wicked!' But, if someone is confident that they are 'righteous', why should they be worried about God destroying the wicked? Similarly, often the people who seem most offended by a Christian speaking out publicly (or putting something on social media) warning about God's judgment and hell are very quick to say they don't believe in hell in any case. Presumably, then, an imaginary hell can cause only imaginary offence?

However, if we take the unmistakable message of the Bible – and of Jesus Christ Himself – with any real seriousness,

---

24.   Psalm 1:5-6.

judgment is an issue we must face up to. And so an absolutely critical question is, who then are the righteous?

Who will stand?

Who are the righteous whom 'the LORD loves'?[25] Who can 'stand in the judgment', as Psalm 1 affirms only the righteous surely shall?[26] Who are those whom God 'preserves' on that day as verse 20 says here, whom He 'saves' (19)?

Well, according to the Bible, it is not, in fact, the morally perfect, if there could really be anyone like that. It is not the spotless, the pious, the religious; it is certainly not the self-righteous virtue-signaler, the proud and the sanctimonious; nor is it those with great pedigree and position or privilege. Who then can it be? We may find the Bible's answer rather surprising, but that answer is articulated very clearly indeed here in this Psalm: The LORD 'is near to all' – notice, *all* – 'who *call* on him' (18), 'who *fear* him' (19), 'who *love* him' (20). His unchangeable covenant promise is to be *near* [emphasis added]– to *fulfil* the heart's desire and to *save* [emphasis added]– all such. He 'preserves' – he watches over forever – '*all* who love him' (20) [emphasis added].

That is why this great king, David, praises the name of his King and his LORD forever. He knows personally the unsearchable greatness and the unchangeable faithfulness of the LORD his God.

That is why, likewise, our great King, great David's greater Son, leads *us* in praise, in the midst of the great congregation of all the redeemed. Jesus, above all others, knows the unfathomable depths of the Father's goodness and grace to those who are His own, for He, above all others, knows the cost – at the heart of heaven itself – of making that grace and mercy known to those who are His. And so Jesus calls us, His brothers and sisters, to join His kingly choir and to sing with

25. Psalm 146:8.
26. Psalm 1:5-6.

Him this great song of salvation. Verses 10-13 at the very heart of this Psalm give us the lyrics to do so.

A Choir of Unquenchable Witness

In singing His song to the world, Christians are called to be a choir of *unquenchable witness* to God our Saviour. The people of this King are a *speaking* people whose praise is marked by *unceasing proclamation* of His everlasting kingdom to all the world.

'All your works shall *declare you*, O LORD' is perhaps a better translation of verse 10. Like in Psalms 8 and 19 he is saying that the whole creation declares and confesses God's glory simply by existing; it shows forth His *praise* in that sense. But it is His saints (10), His own people, who alone truly know His saving wonders and therefore can most truly bless His name. It is the Christian believer, alone, who can sing,

> Praise, my soul, the King of Heaven;
> to his feet your tribute bring.
> ransomed, healed, restored, forgiven,
> who like me his praise should sing?[27]

We are the people who have a share in this wondrous story to sing, of a God of unsearchable greatness, a *God* whose kingdom power and gracious glory have now been revealed to us supremely in the great *King*, our LORD Jesus Christ. We are the ones who have a gospel of unchangeable faithfulness, which continues today as He still preserves this earth, and people's lives, so that the promise of His eternal salvation will reach the very ends of this earth – through us. This is what Jesus has promised – a gospel which shall be proclaimed to the ends of the earth so that *all* who will call on Him, and fear Him, and love Him, He *will* save, and will watch over for ever and ever.

---

27. Henry Francis Lyte (1793-1847).

The calling of the church.

This is the glorious calling of the Christian church. This is what it means to be a Christian: to join the choir of our great God and King, the LORD Jesus Christ, and thus 'to bless his name' the way He loves to be blessed, by speaking and making known to the people of this world His mighty deeds and His saving mercies. It is through this that many will hear of Him, and will want to come and join this choir, to sing with us, forever, of the glory of His eternal kingdom.

And the bigger the choir, the greater the sound! This choir and this song is for *all* the saints, for all who are His own. Every believer is called to join the choir of our great King: 'all the saints shall bless you' (10). And this is how we are to sing:

They shall *speak* of the glory of your kingdom
    and *tell* of your power,
to *make known* to the children of man your mighty deeds,
    and the glorious splendor of your kingdom.
Your kingdom is an everlasting kingdom,
    and your dominion endures throughout
    all generations [emphasis added].

This is *our* story, and this is *our* song! So may it be heard from your lips, and mine in our lives as we go about our business, in our work, in our classrooms, in the streets, and with our friends and neighbours. May it be our song always, until our LORD Himself comes to lead all who belong to Him in that great chorus of praise, forever and ever! Amen.

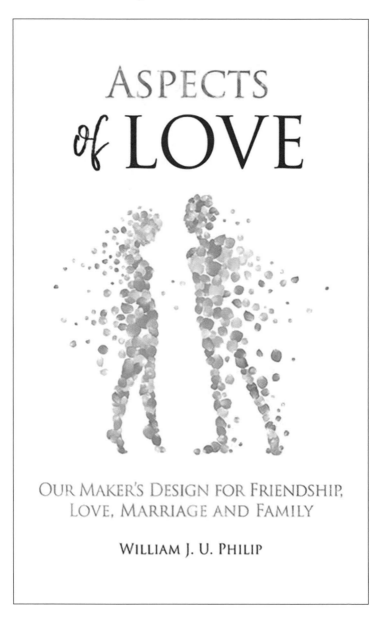

ASPECTS
of LOVE

OUR MAKER'S DESIGN FOR FRIENDSHIP, LOVE, MARRIAGE AND FAMILY

WILLIAM J. U. PHILIP

Aspects of Love

Our Maker's design for friendship, love, marriage and family

by William J. U. Philip

We all want, and need, to love and to be loved. We are made in the image of God, who is love. Healthy loving is at the very heart of true human flourishing, but human life is full of love gone wrong – marriages break down, relationships with family members are strained, loneliness is an ever–increasing problem. This book delves into what the Bible has to say on relationships – friendship, love, marriage, sex and family – and how to guard them and keep them

Trained first as a physician and now entrusted with the care of souls, the author is uniquely placed to address matters healthy and holy. Providing both diagnosis and cure, he shows how an understanding of God's love for us lays the foundation for loving and being loved.

Alistair Begg

Senior Pastor, Parkside Church, Chagrin Falls, Ohio

Christian Focus Publications

Our mission statement –

STAYING FAITHFUL

In dependence upon God we seek to impact the world through literature faithful to His infallible Word, the Bible. Our aim is to ensure that the Lord Jesus Christ is presented as the only hope to obtain forgiveness of sin, live a useful life and look forward to heaven with Him.

Our books are published in four imprints:

CHRISTIAN
FOCUS

Popular works including biographies, commentaries, basic doctrine and Christian living.

CHRISTIAN
HERITAGE

Books representing some of the best material from the rich heritage of the church.

MENTOR

Books written at a level suitable for Bible College and seminary students, pastors, and other serious readers. The imprint includes commentaries, doctrinal studies, examination of current issues and church history.

CF4•K

Children's books for quality Bible teaching and for all age groups: Sunday school curriculum, puzzle and activity books; personal and family devotional titles, biographies and inspirational stories – because you are never too young to know Jesus!

Christian Focus Publications Ltd,
Geanies House, Fearn, Ross-shire,
IV20 1TW, Scotland, United Kingdom.
www.christianfocus.com